Flying Colors 2

An Expert Level Coloring Adventure • Music & Arts

ILLUSTRATED BY Jennifer Leigh Allison

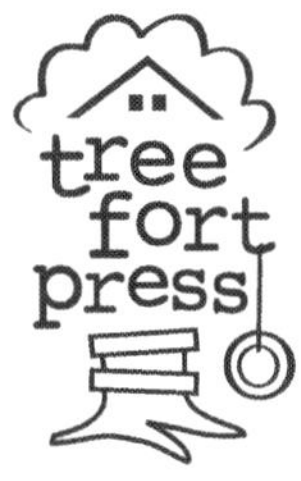

Flying Colors 2: Music & Arts

ISBN-10: 0990771237

ISBN-13: 978-0-9907712-3-4

Published by

Tree Fort Press

Johns Creek, Georgia

www.jenniferleighallison.com

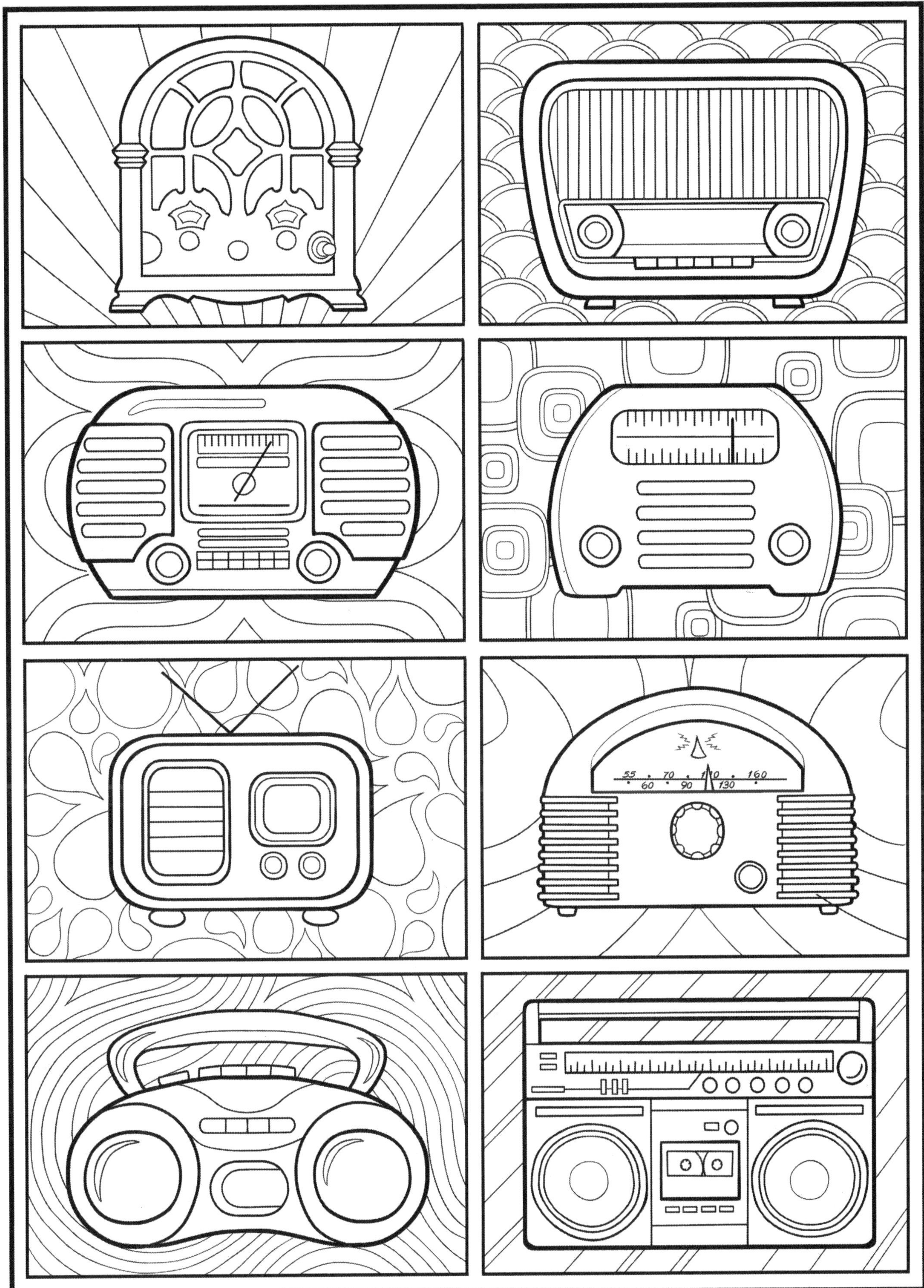
55
70
160
60
90
130

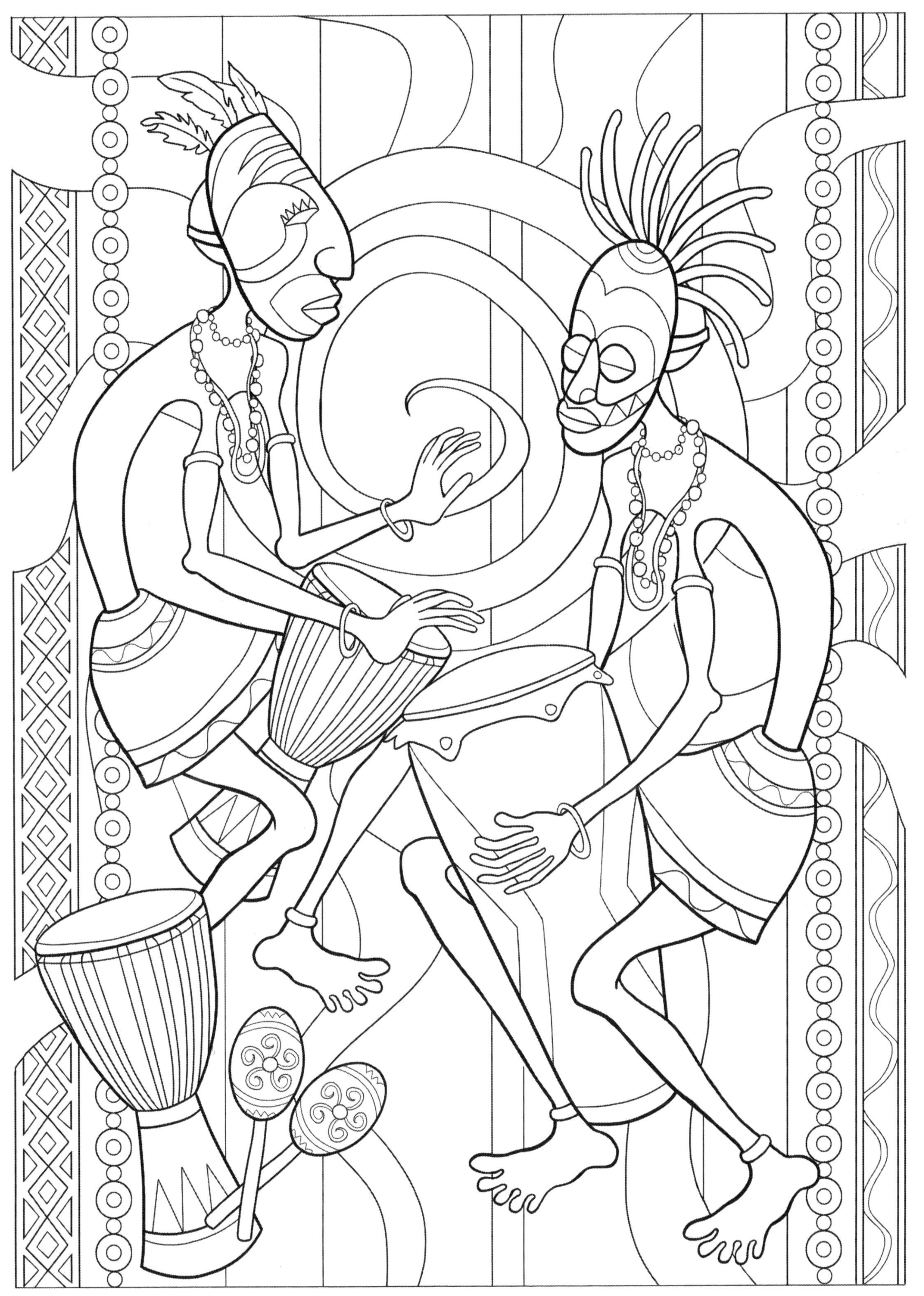

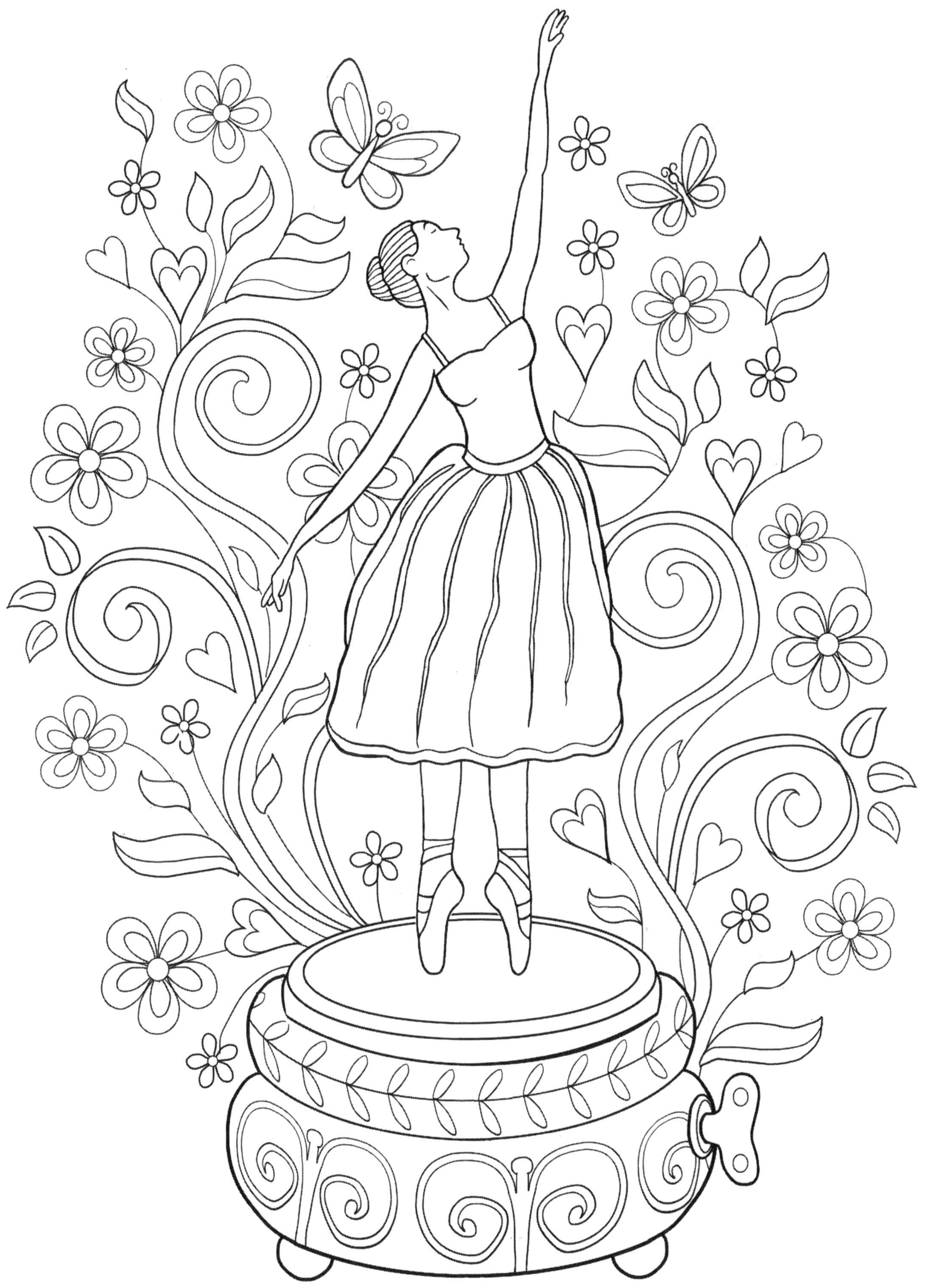

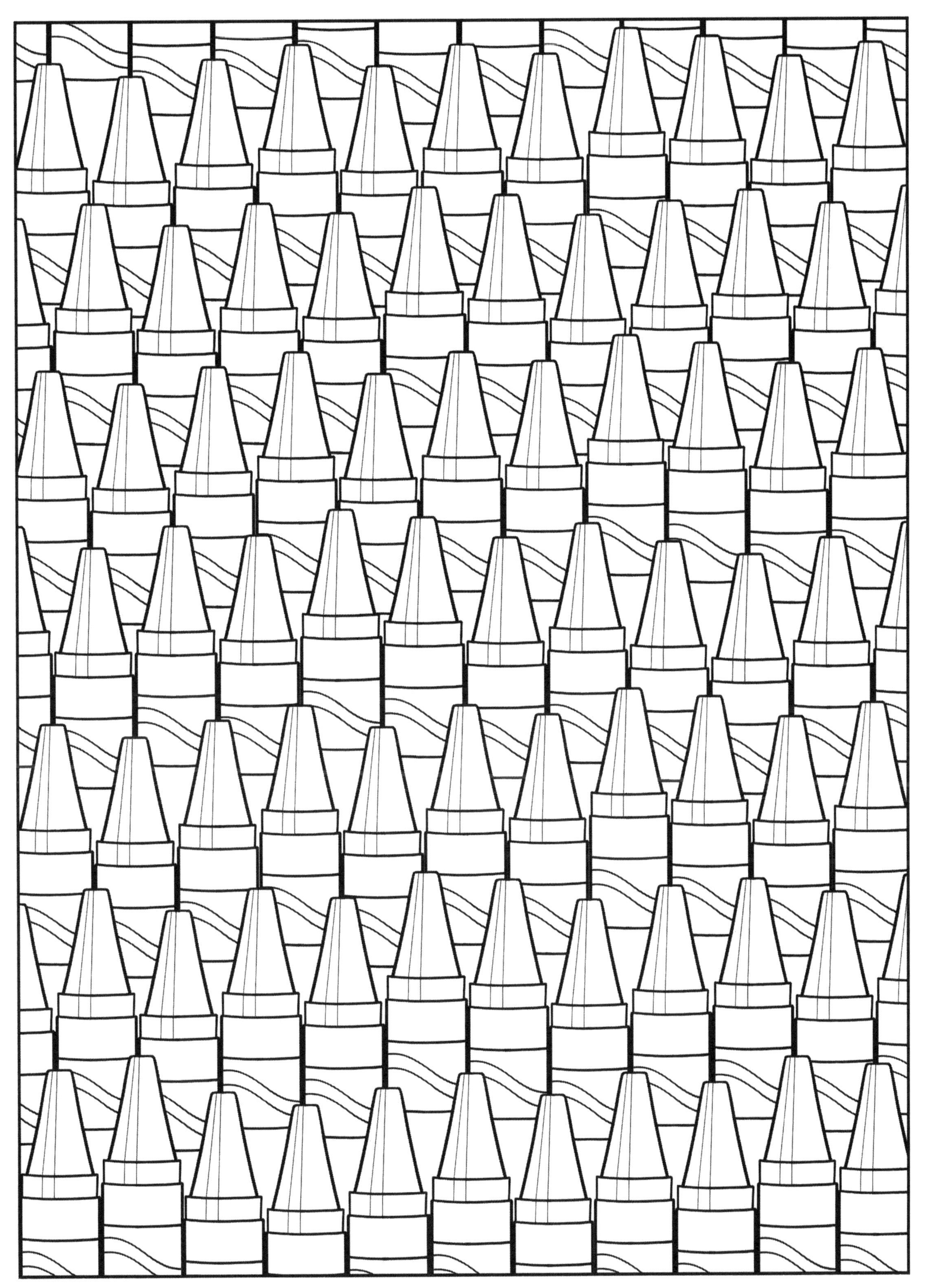

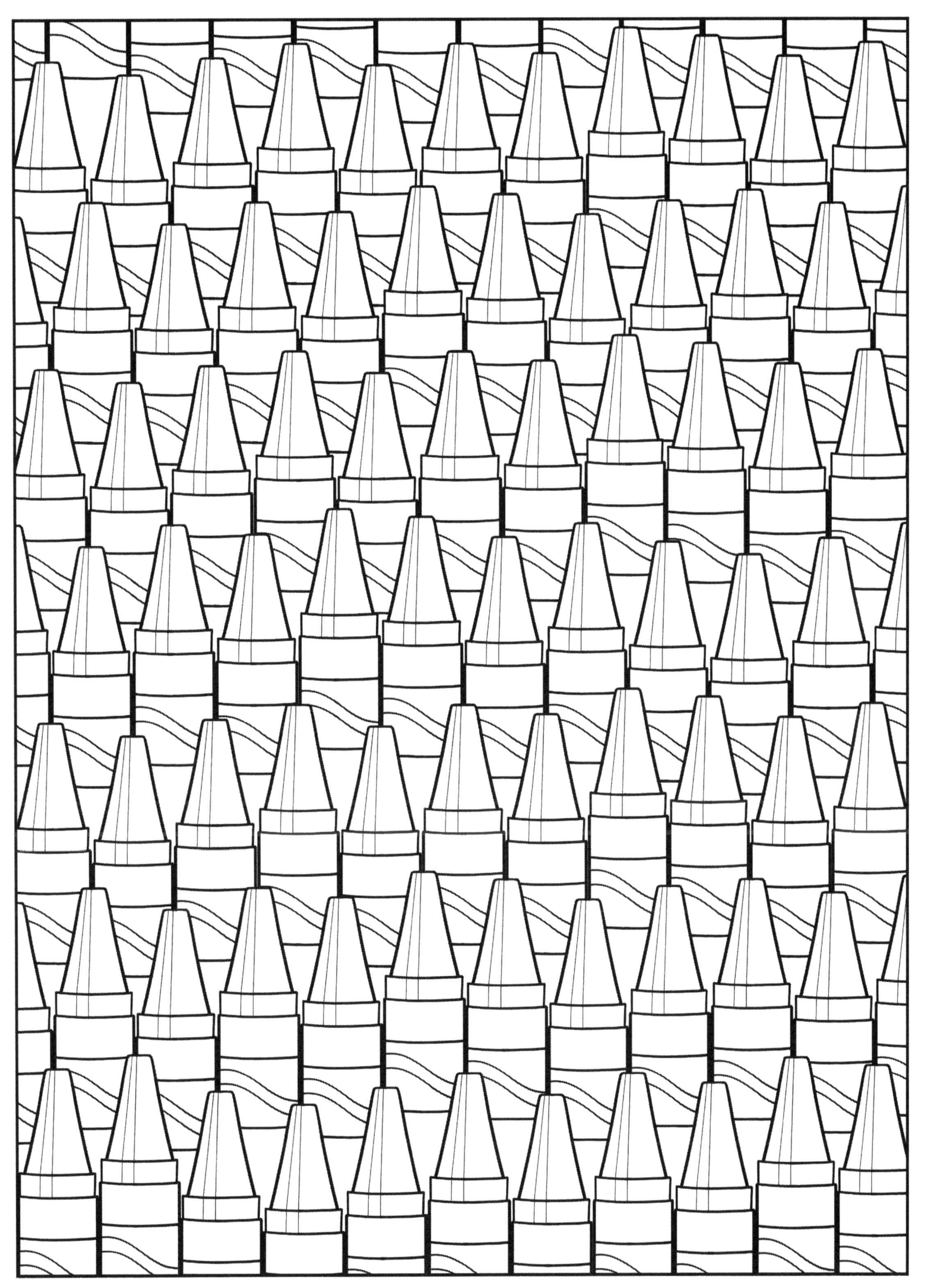

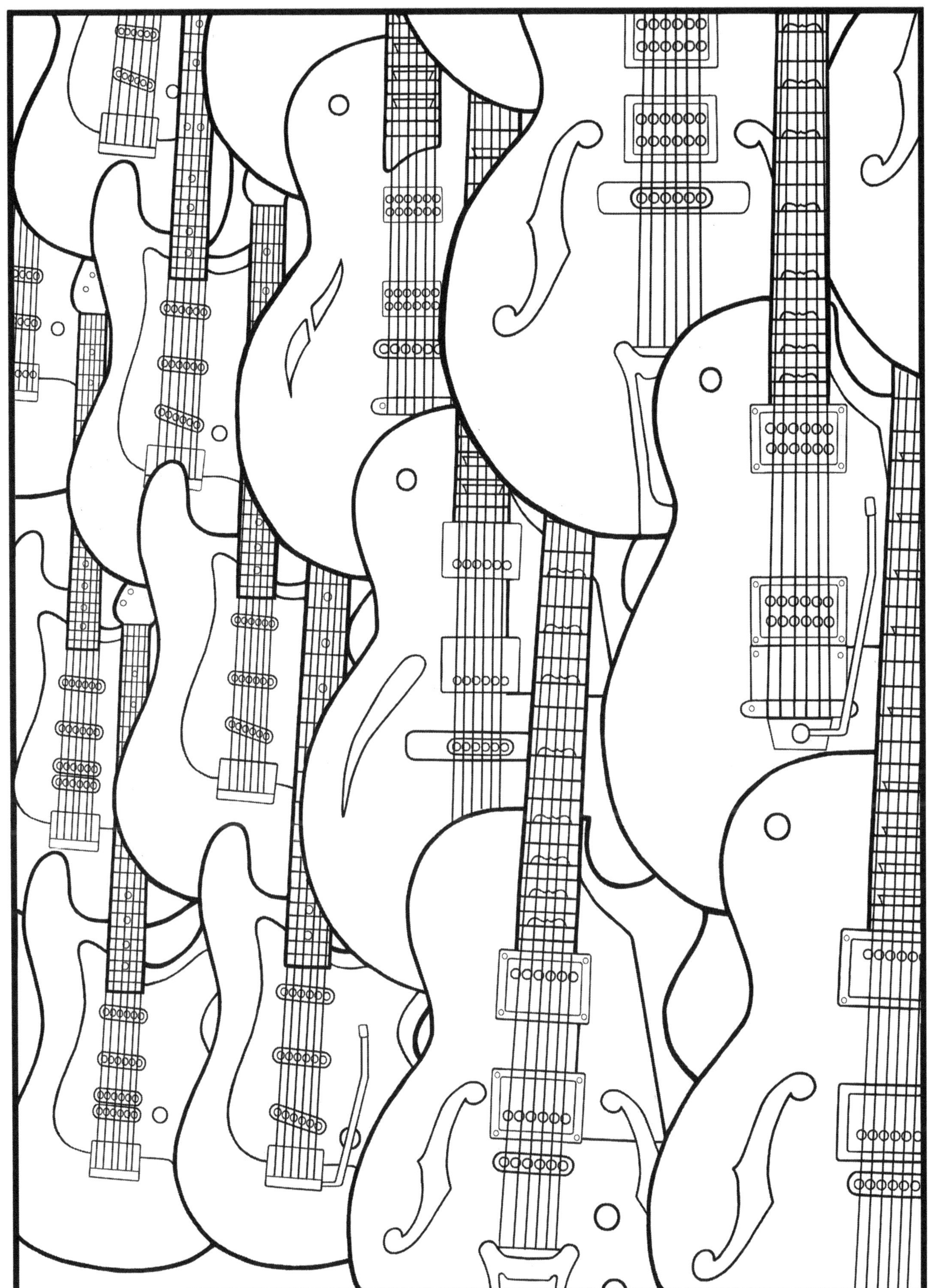

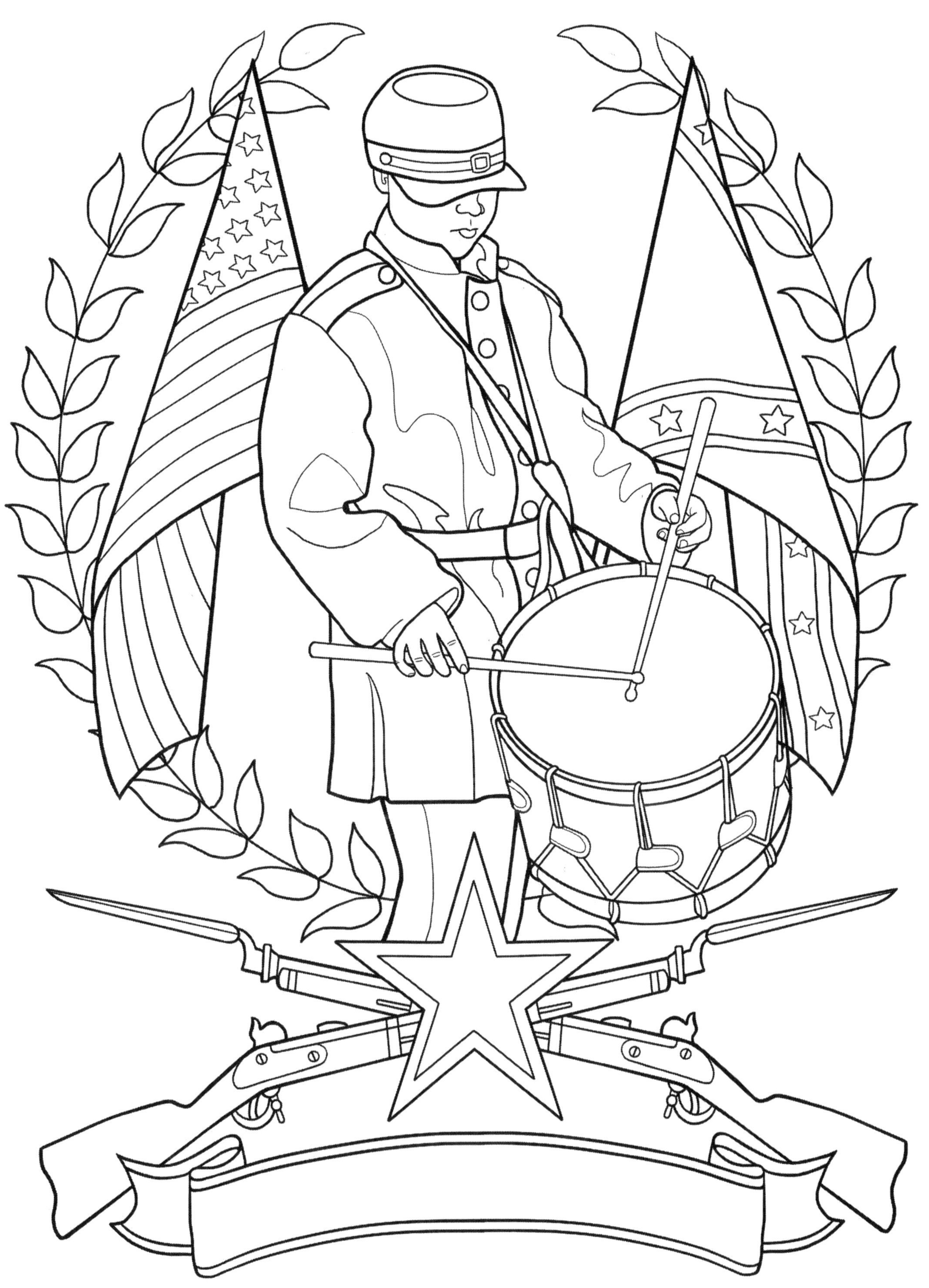

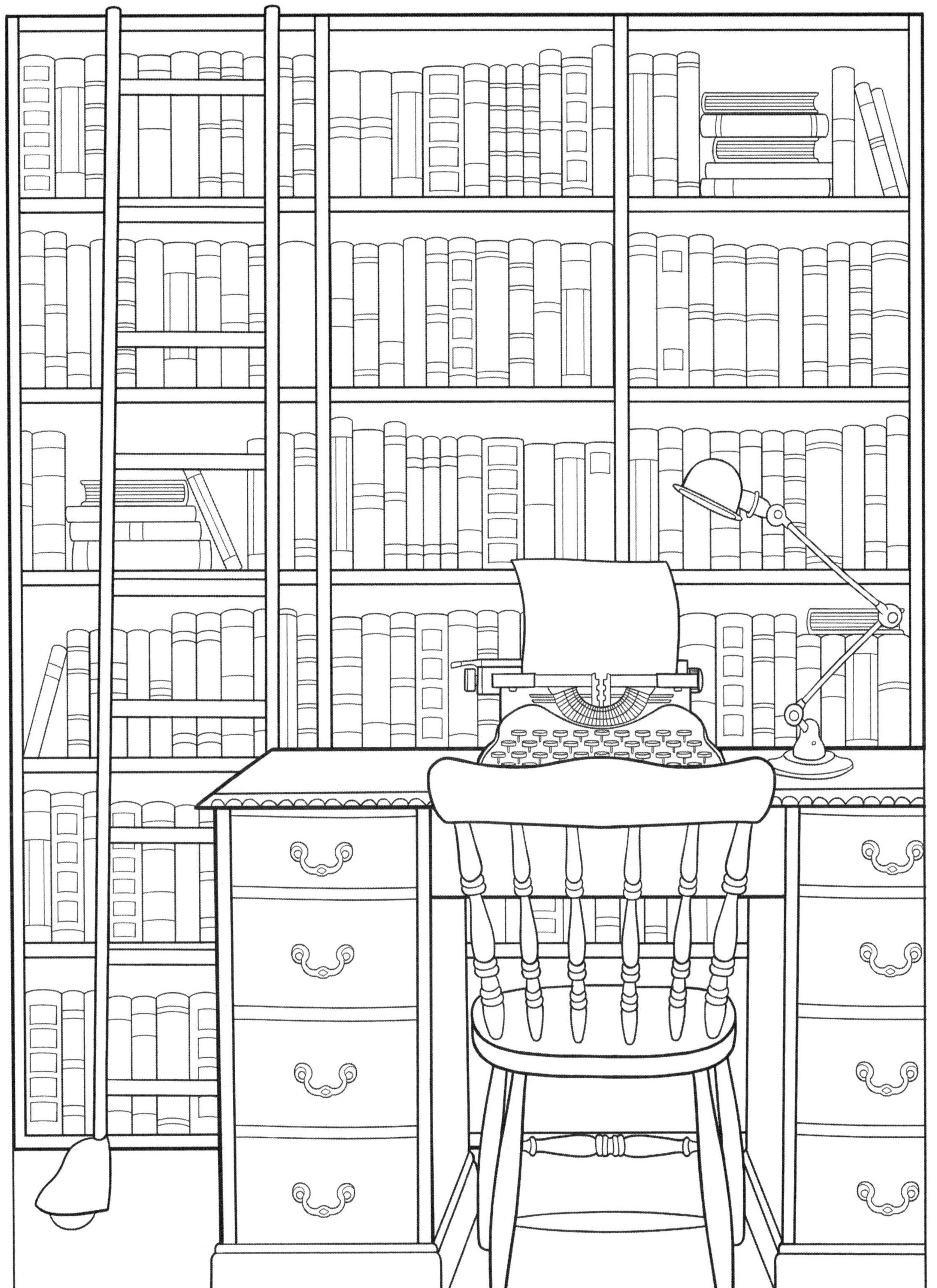

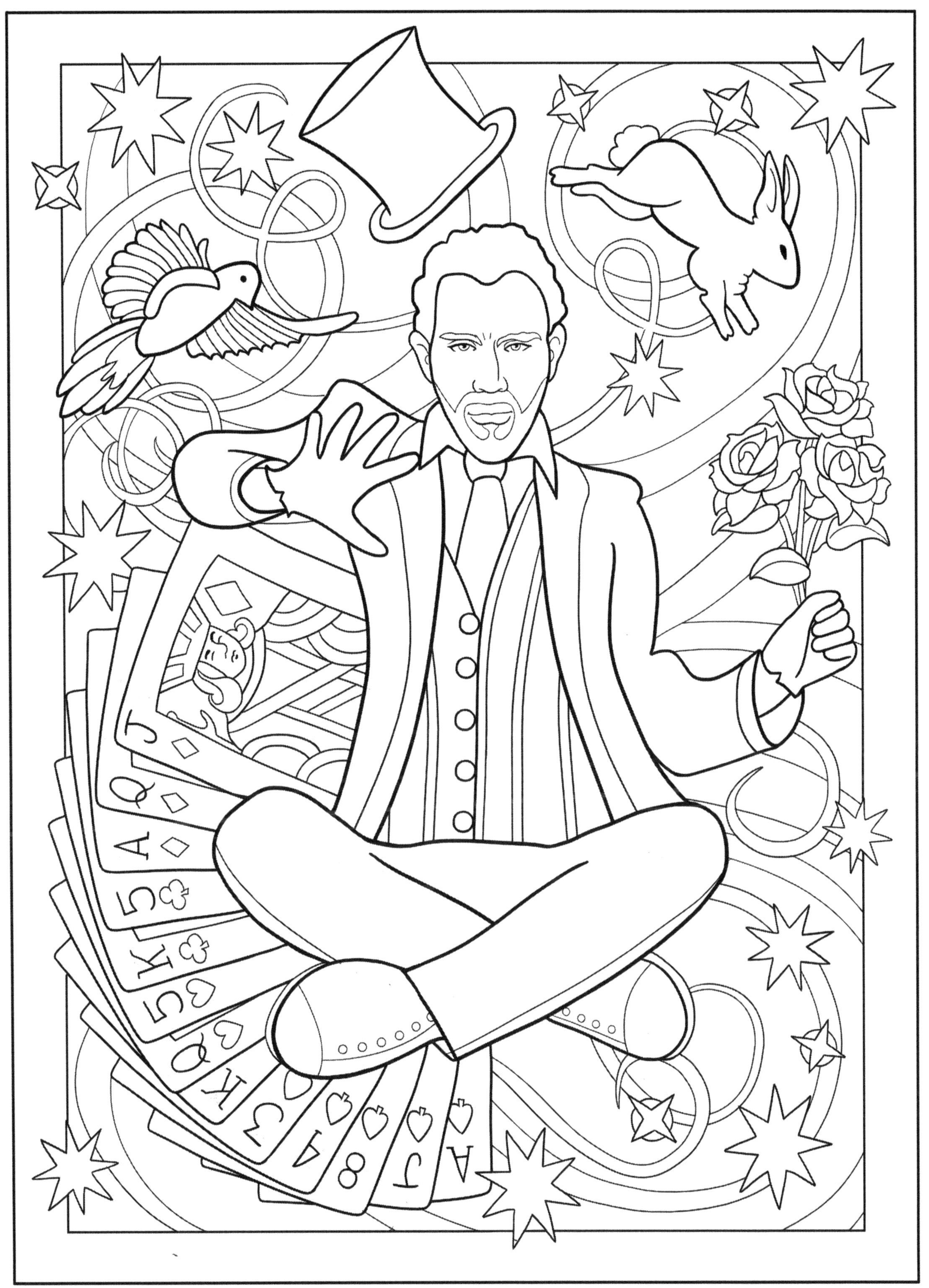

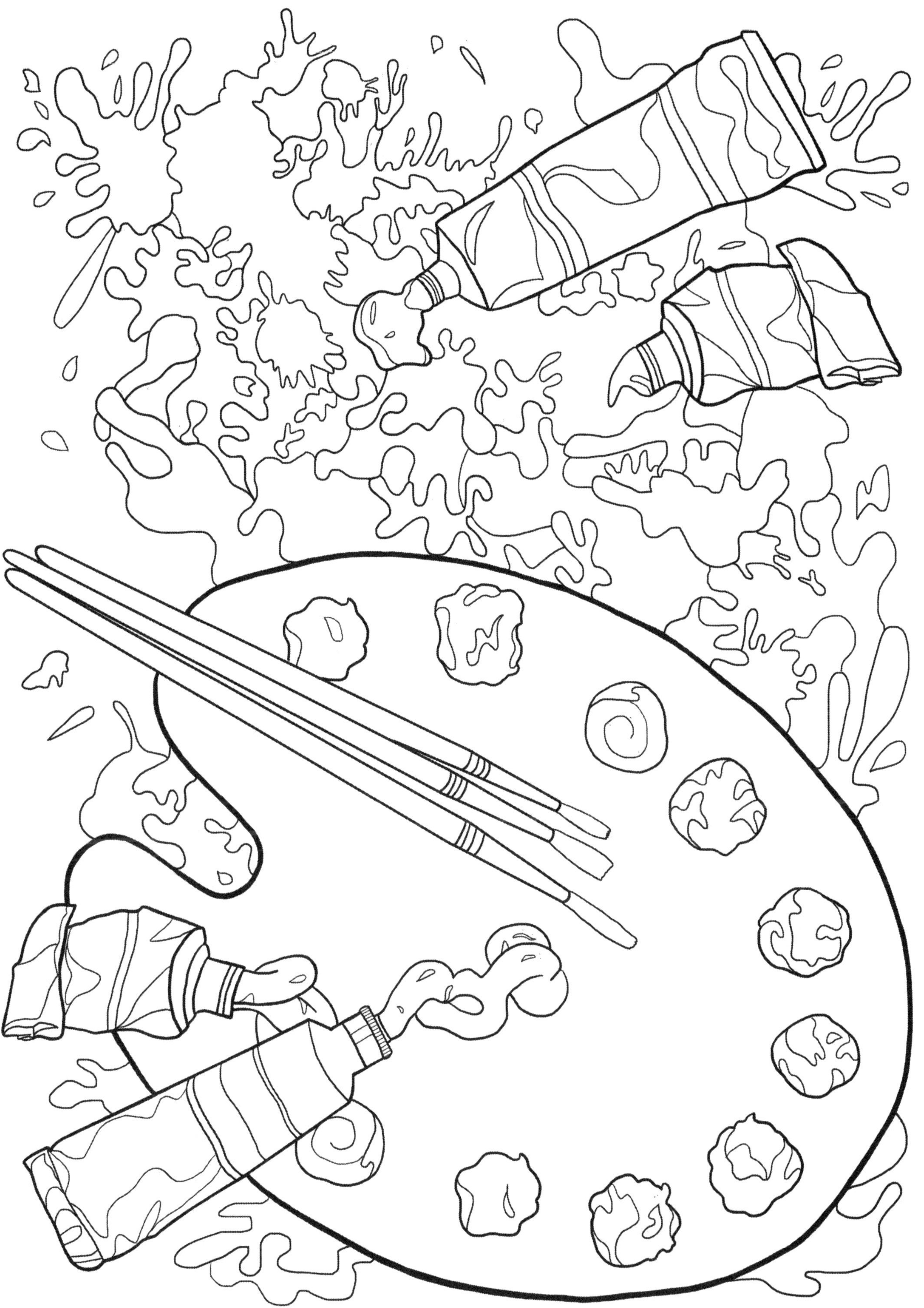

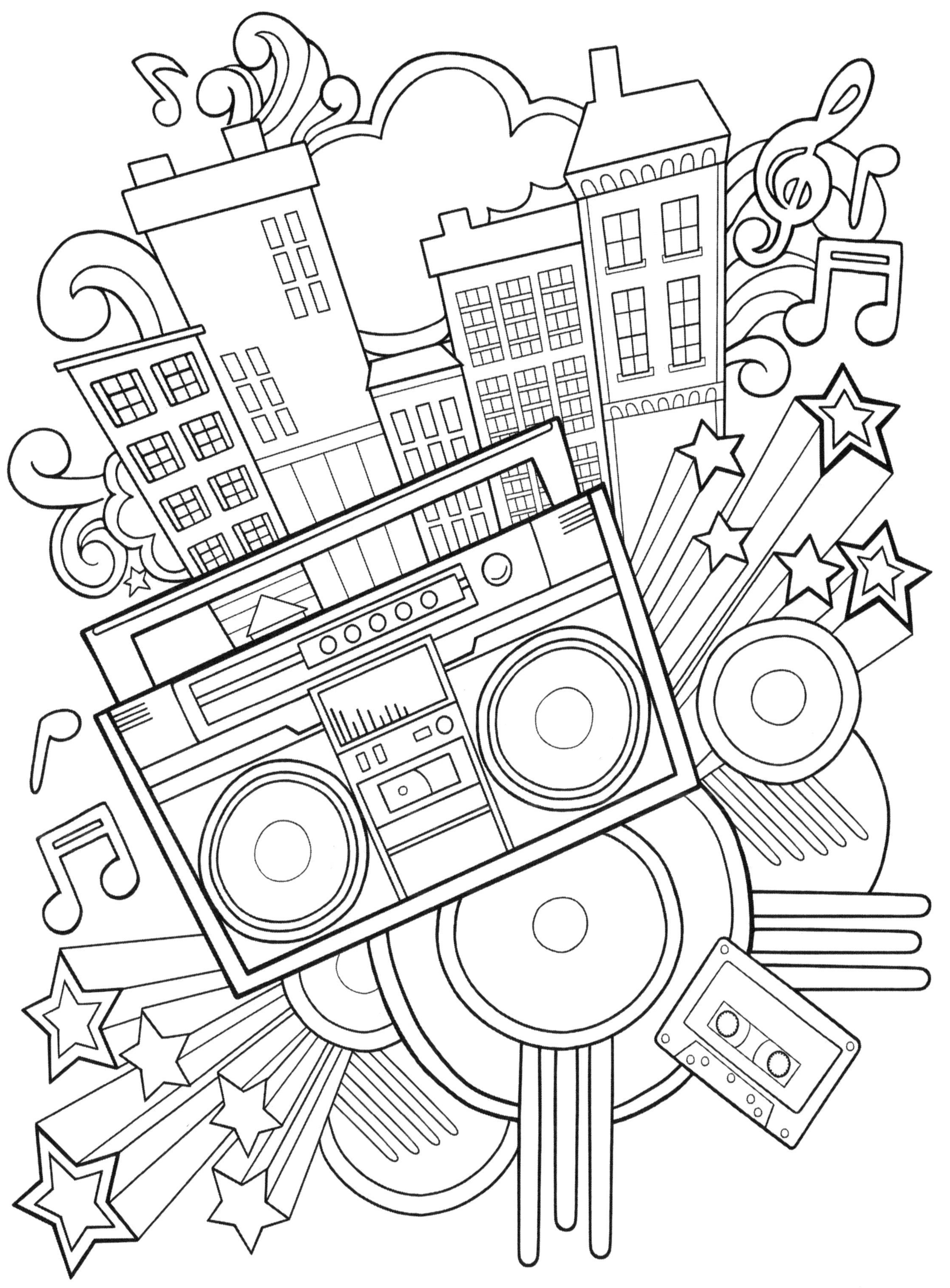

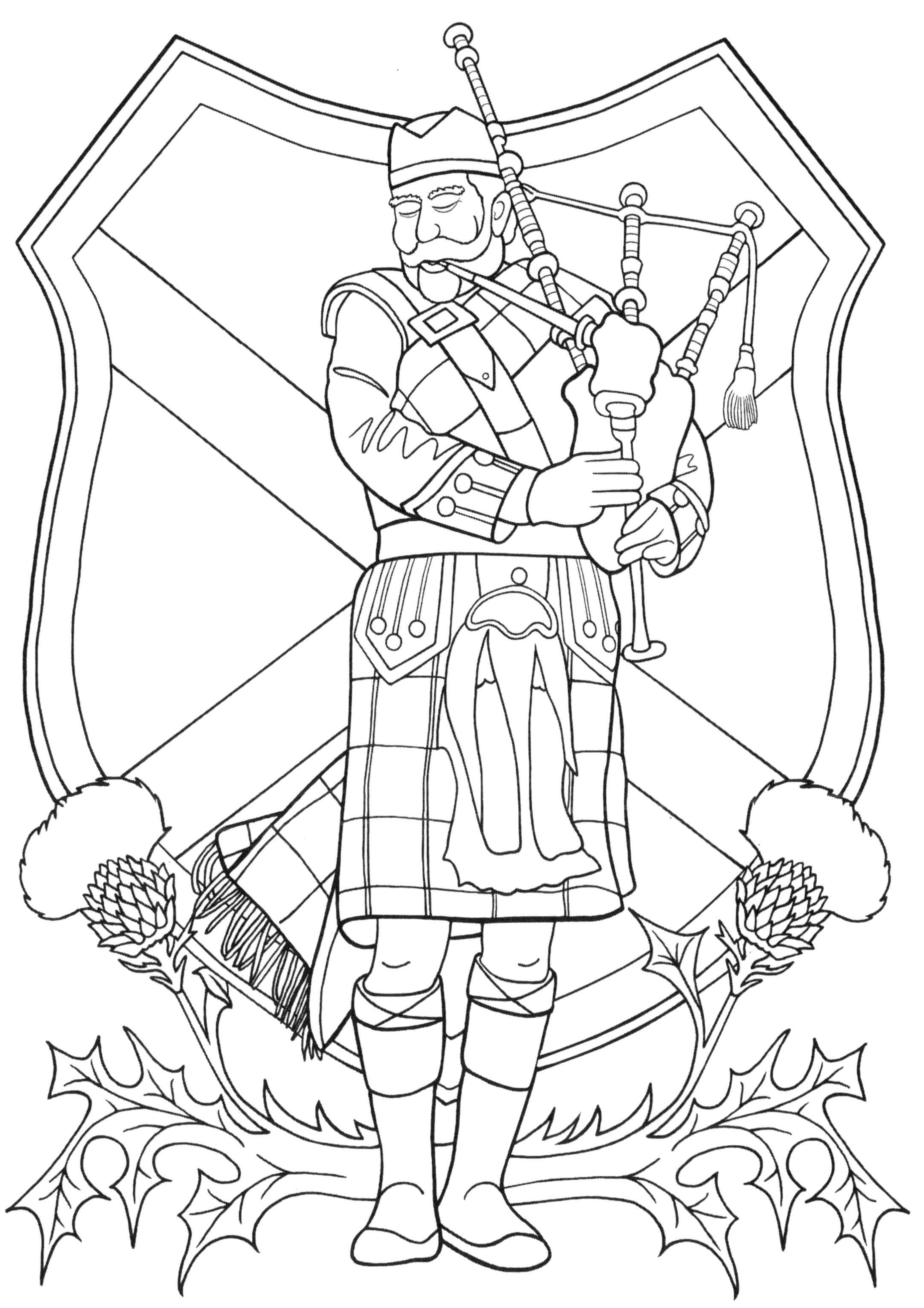

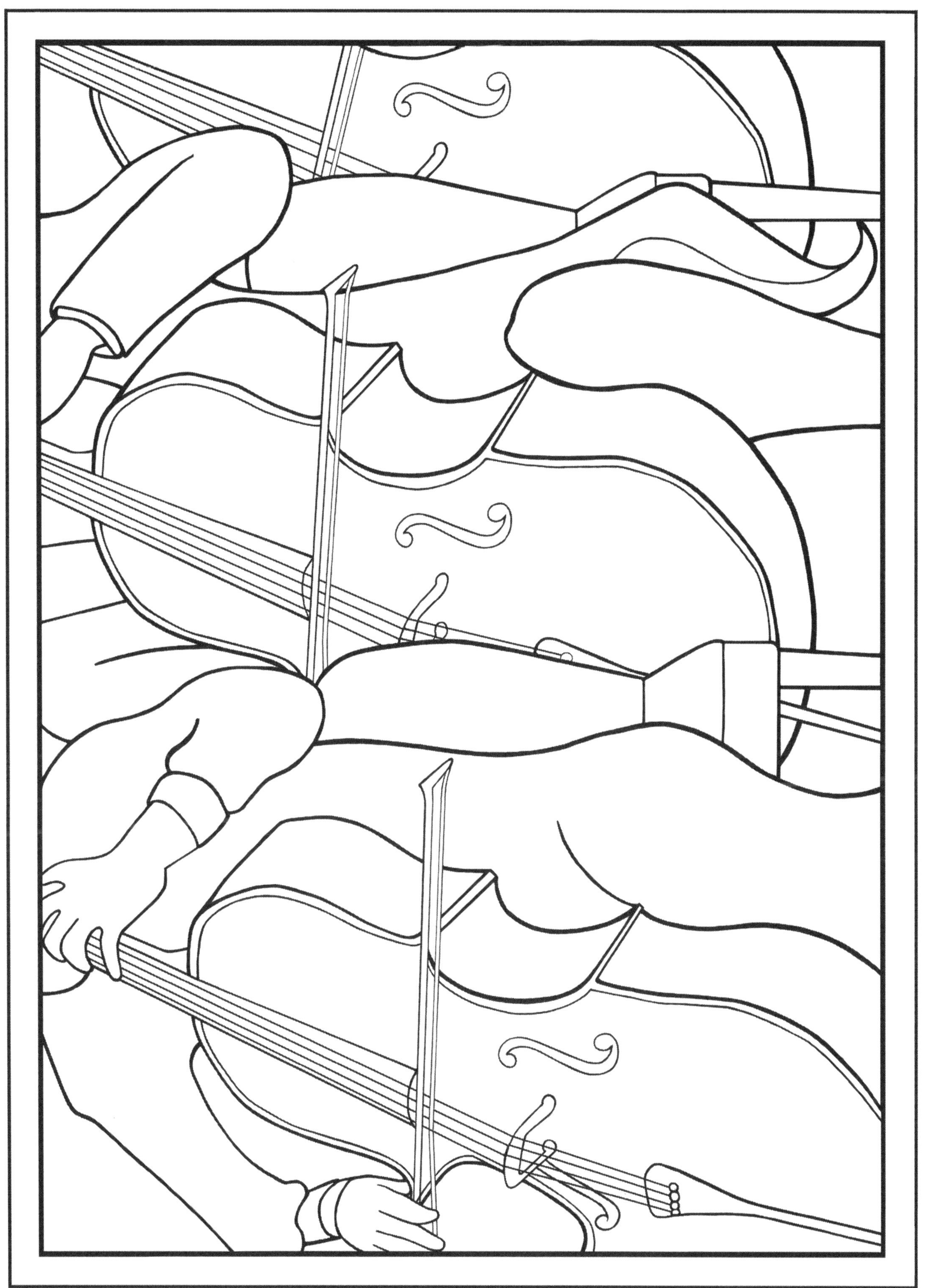

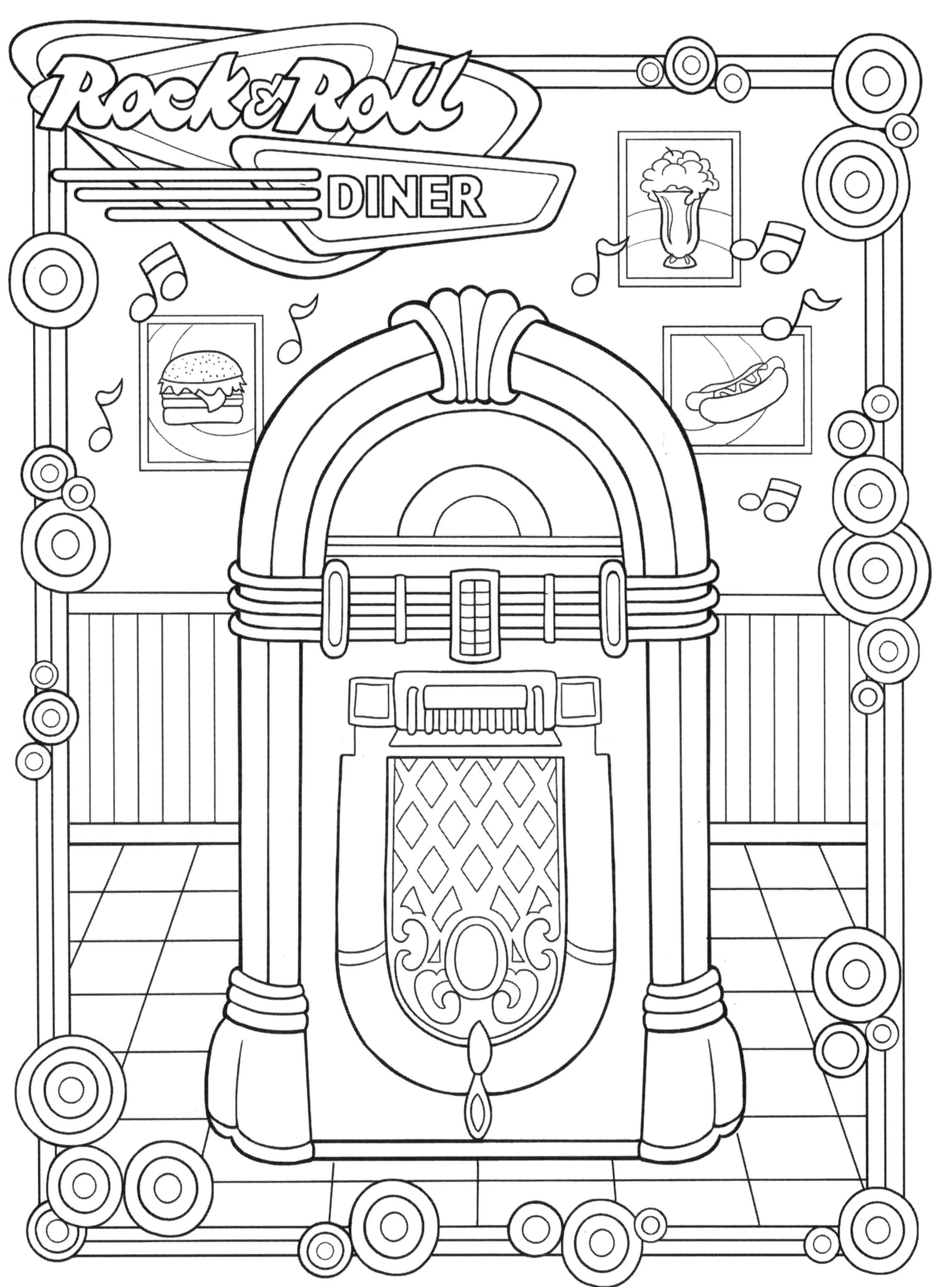
Rock&Roll
DINER

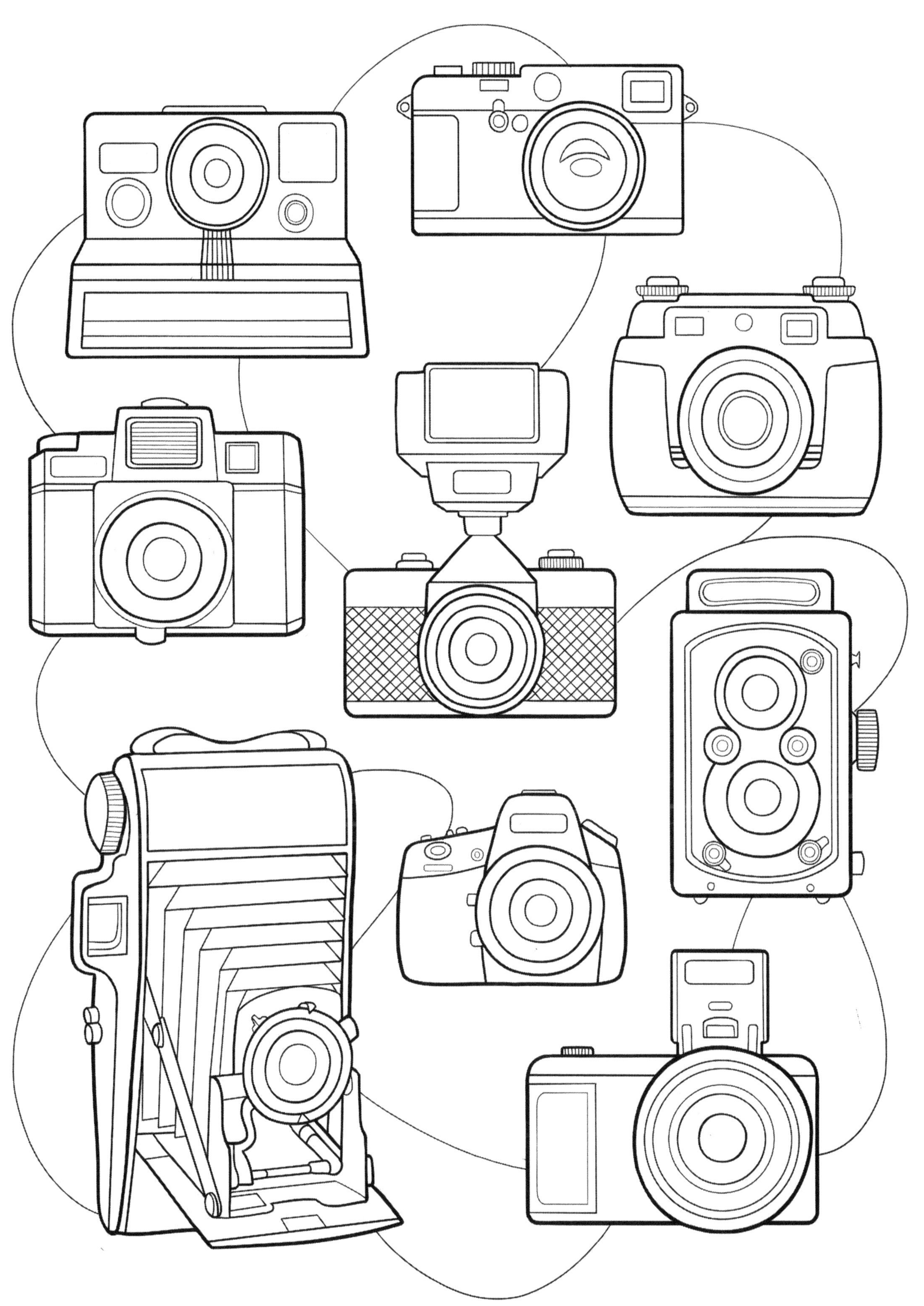

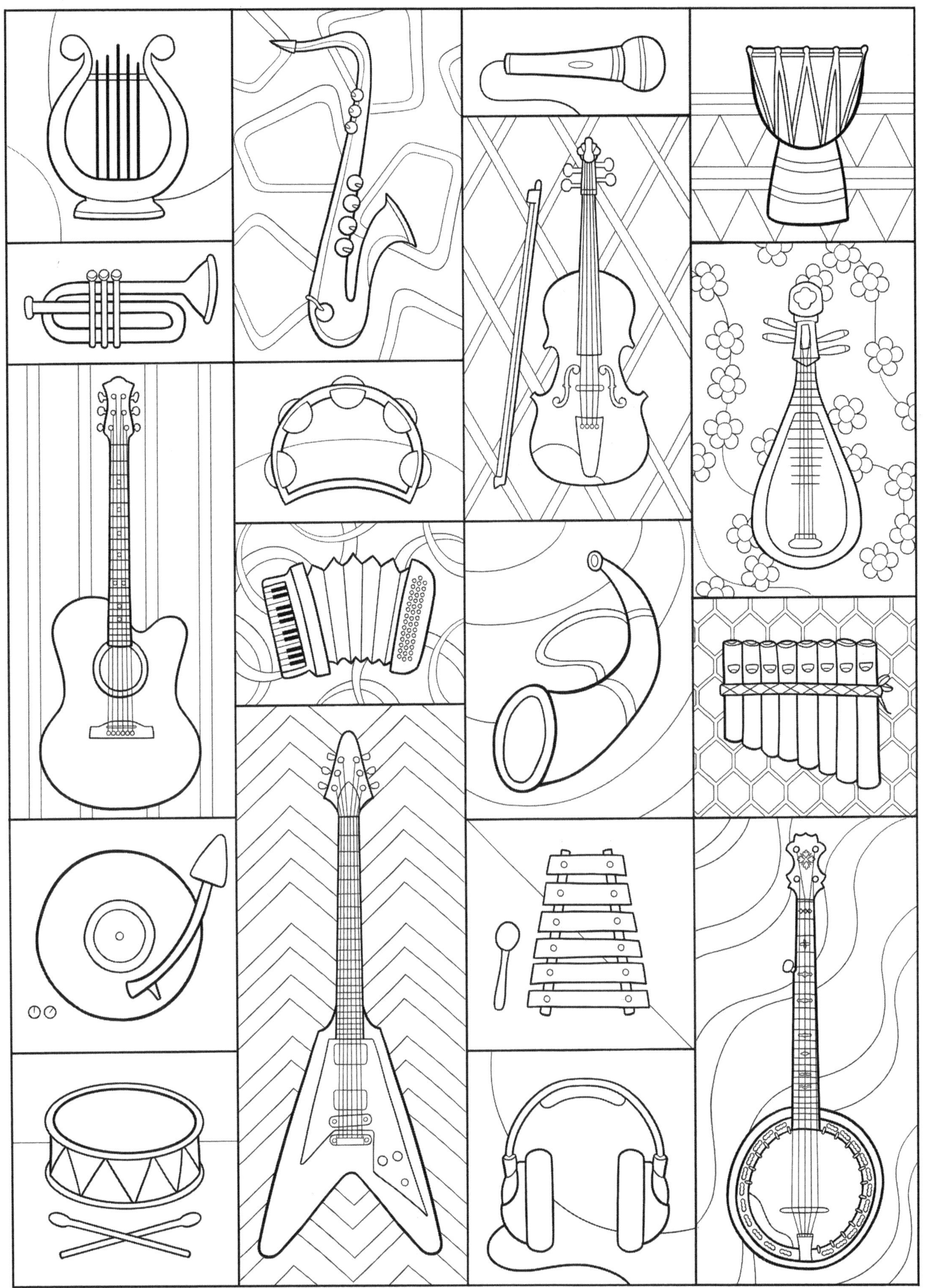

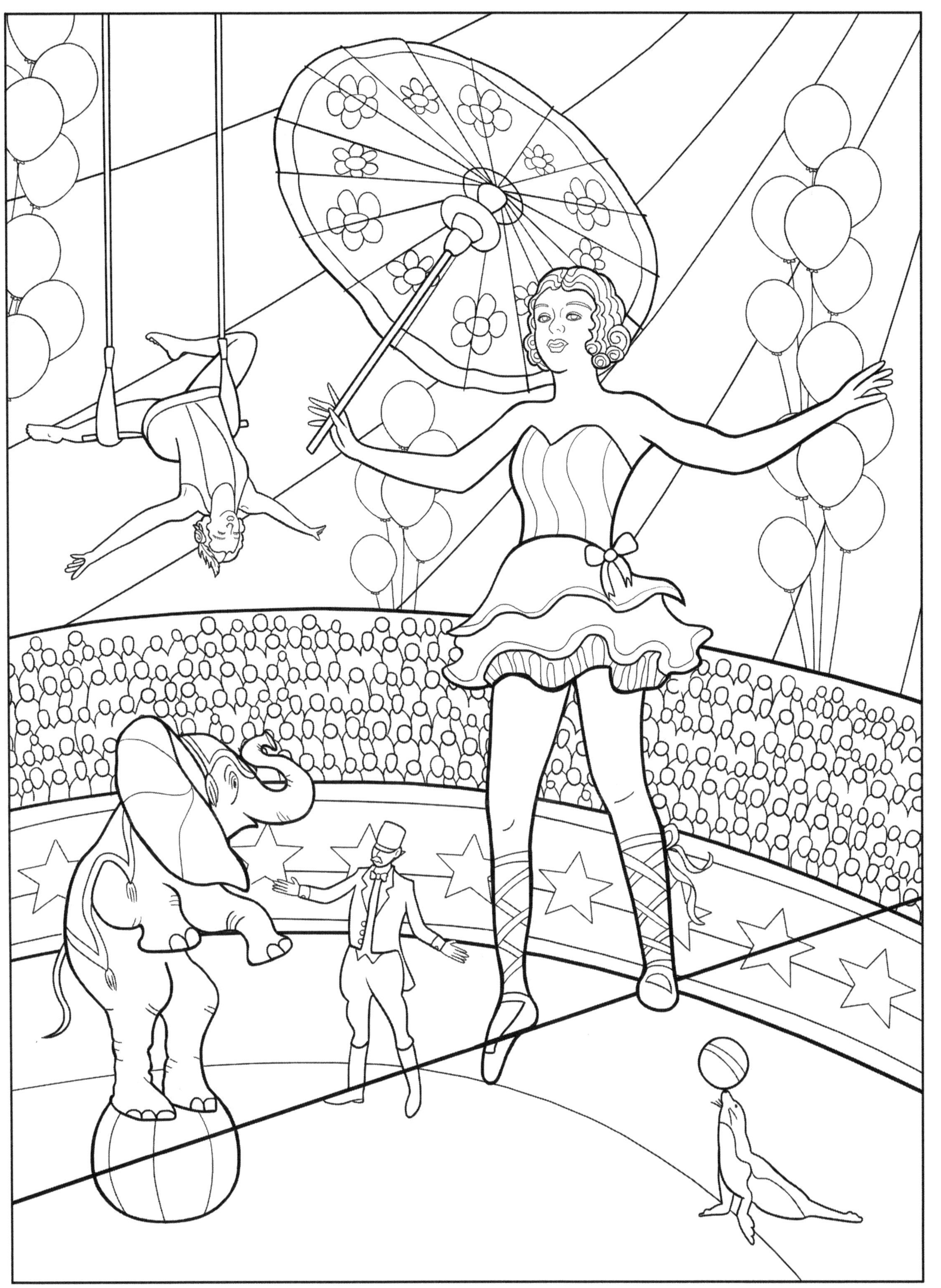

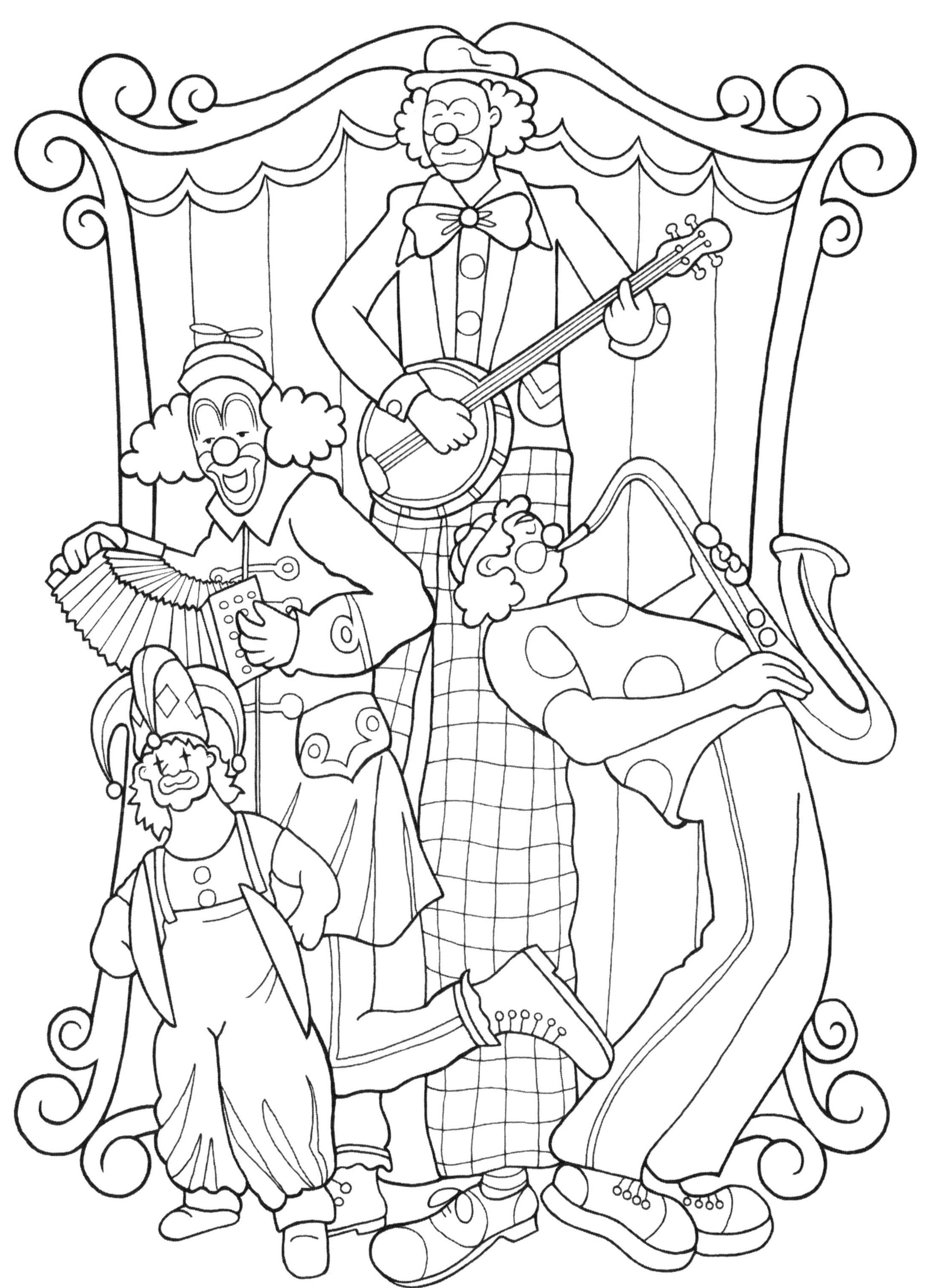

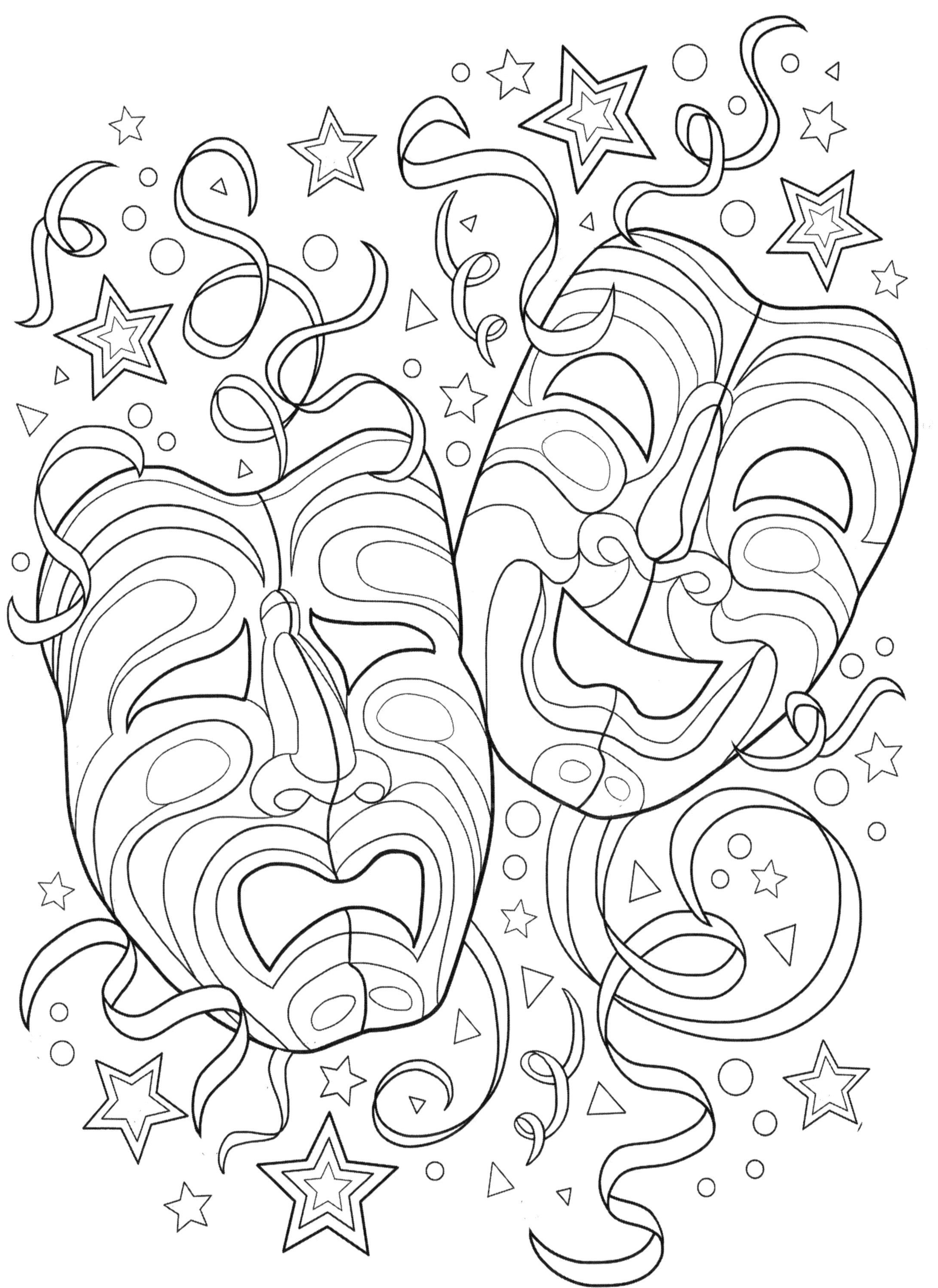

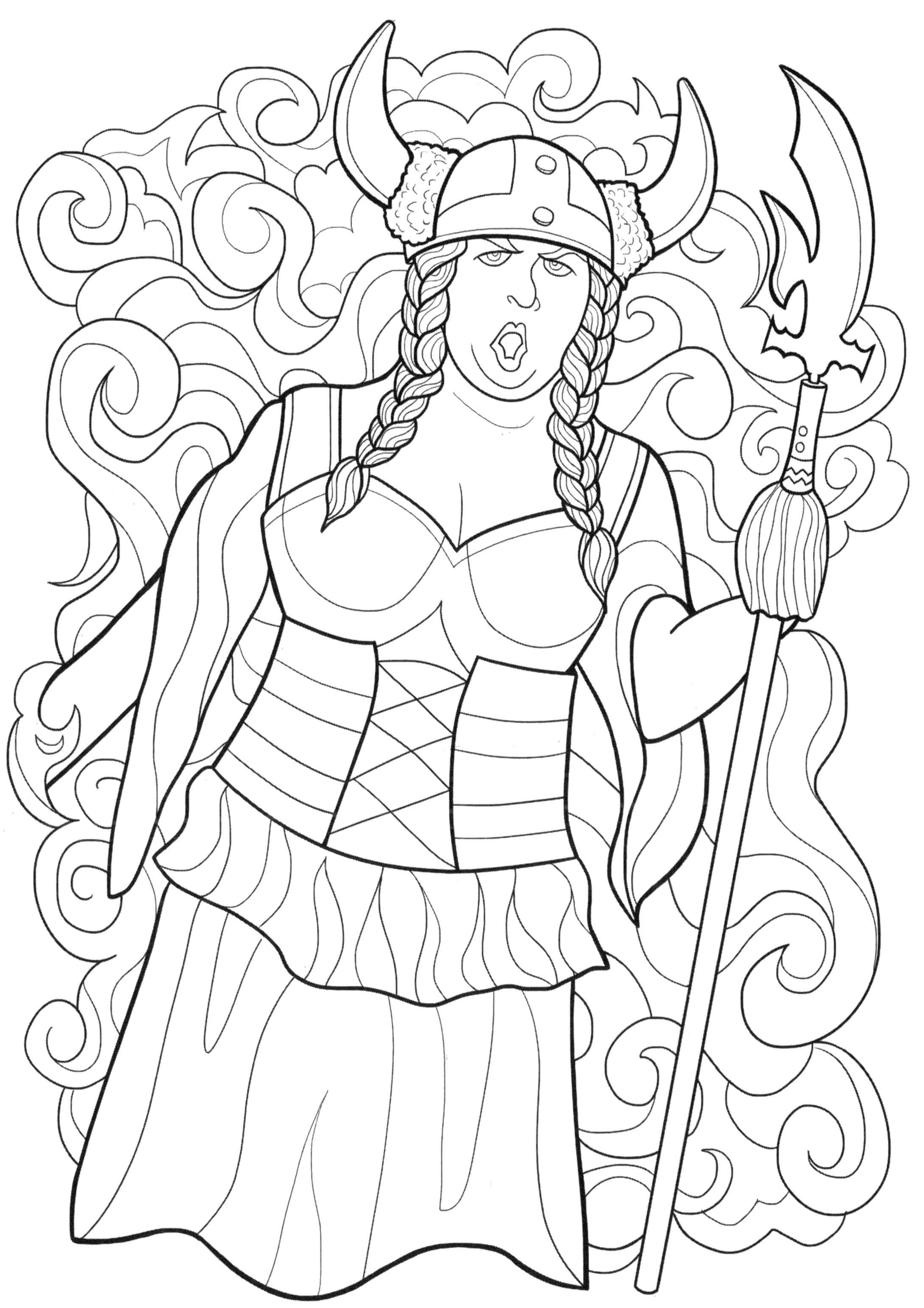

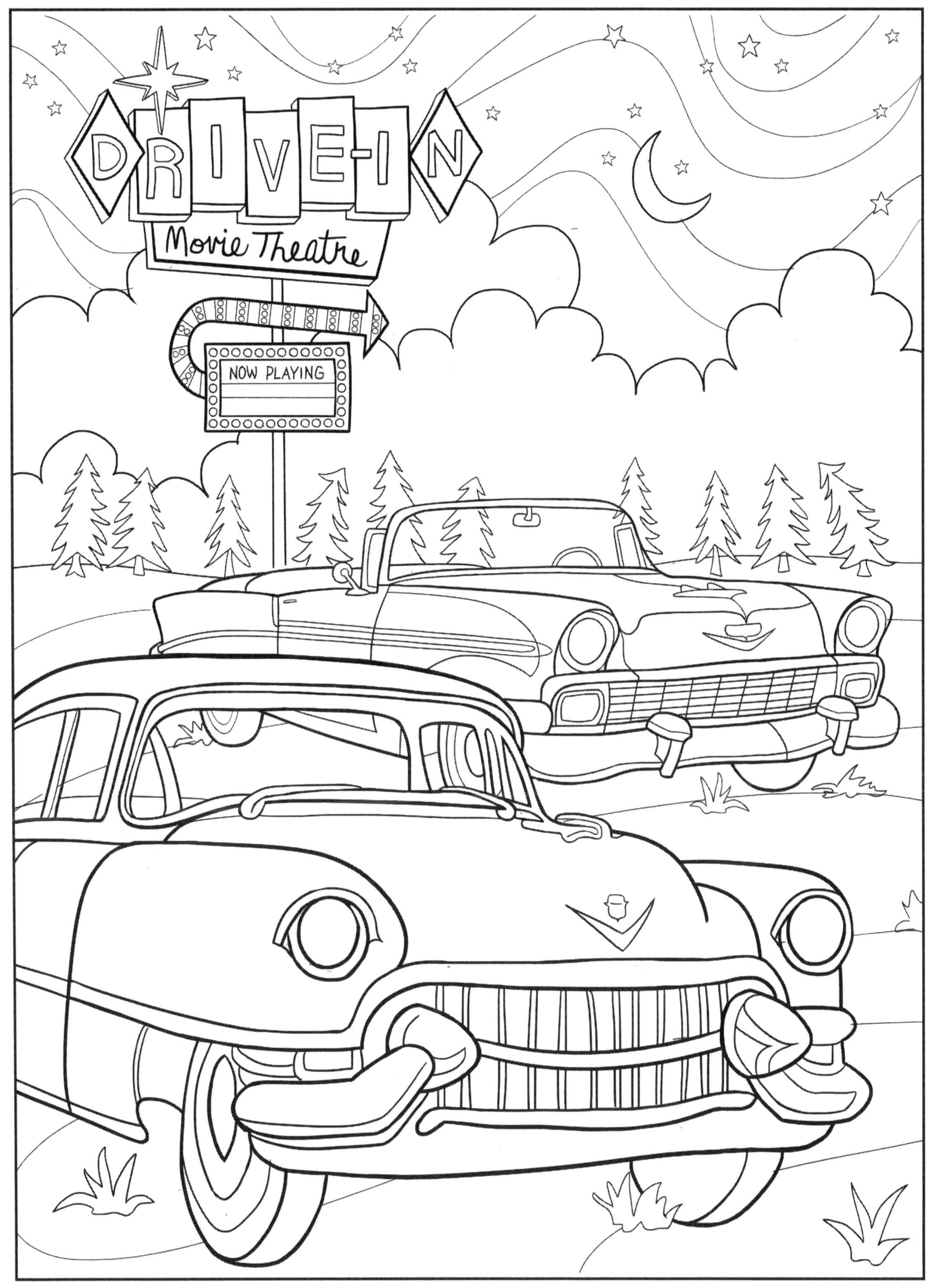
DRIVE-IN
Movie Theatre
NOW PLAYING

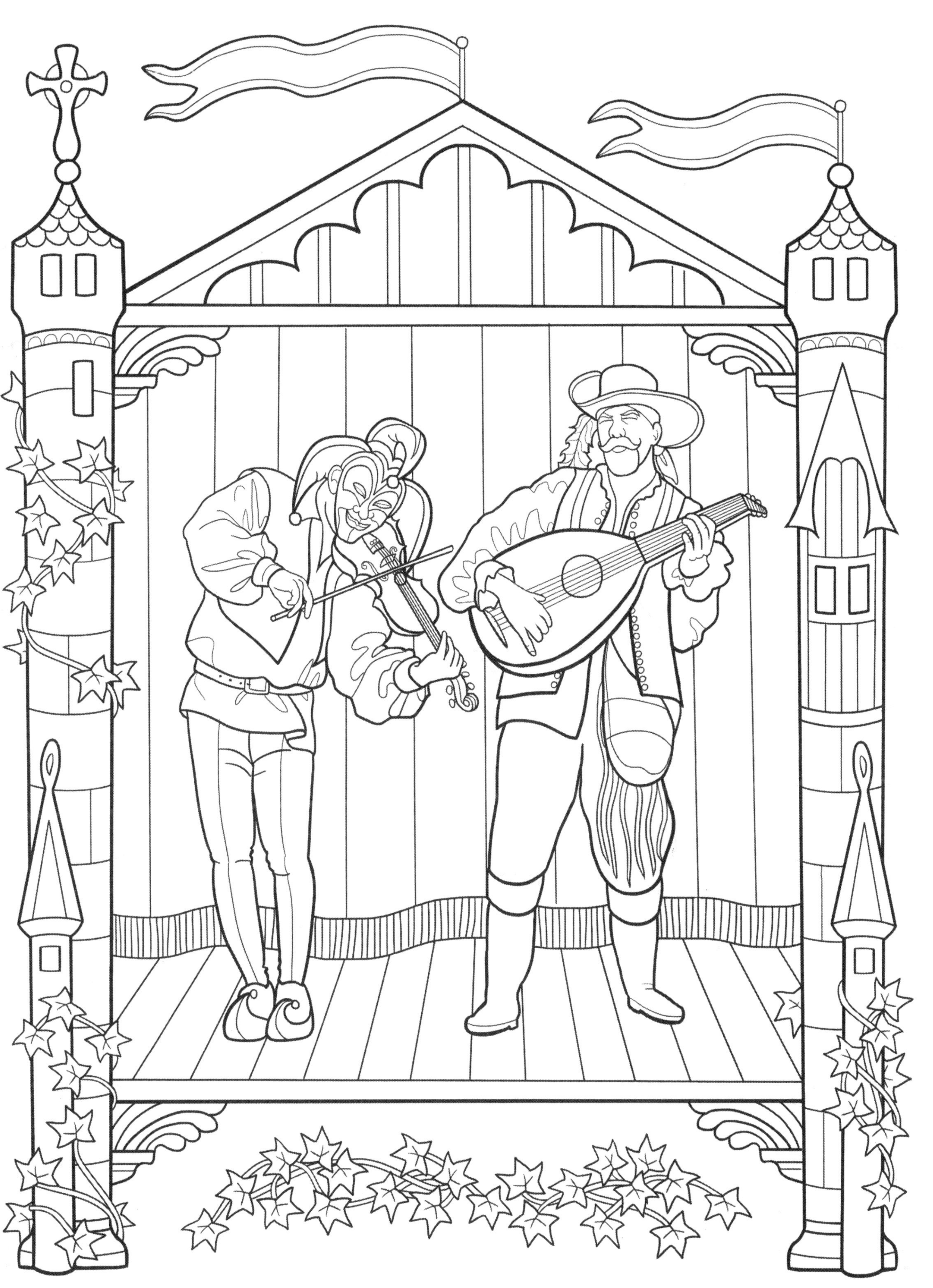

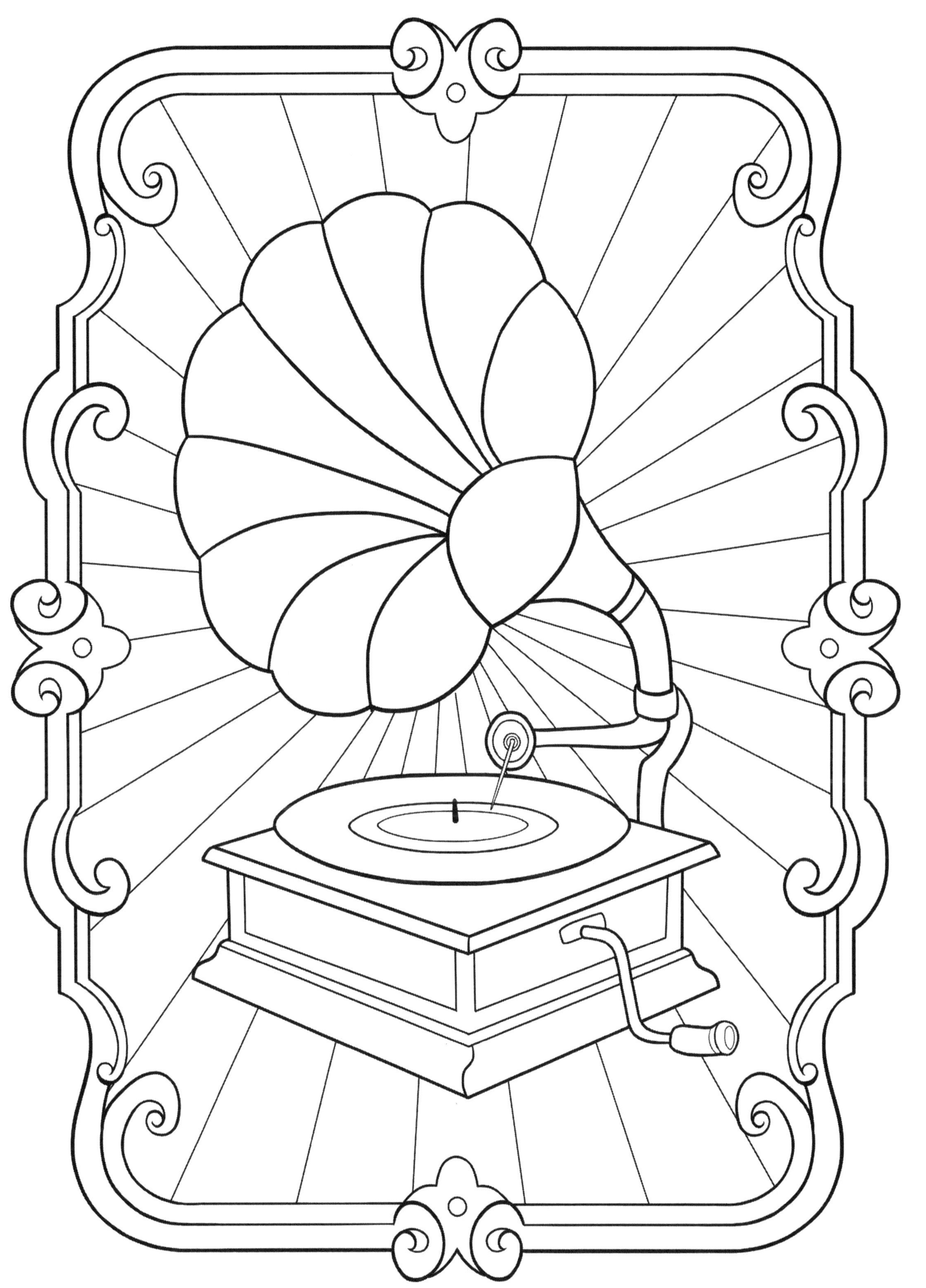

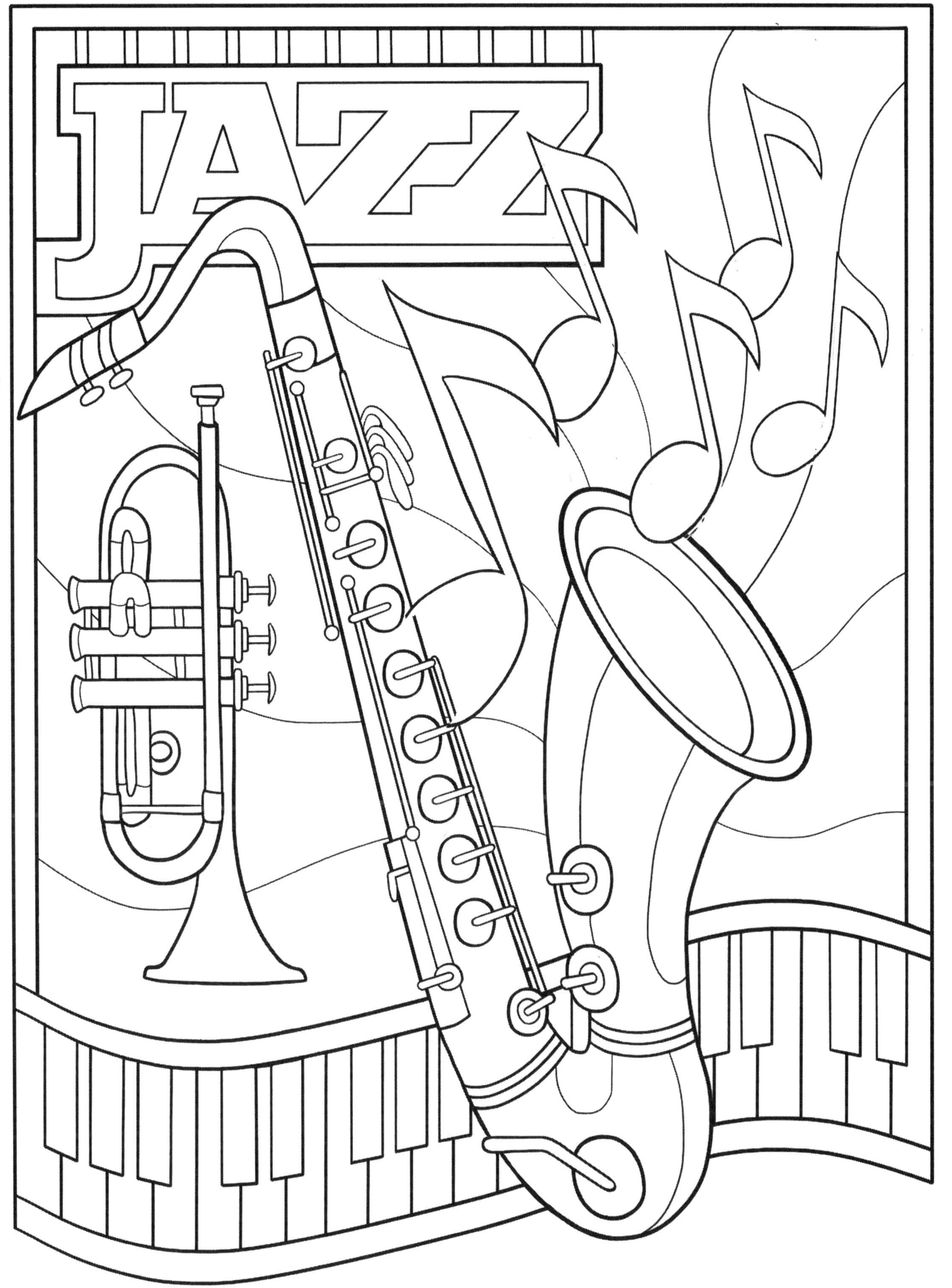
JAZZ

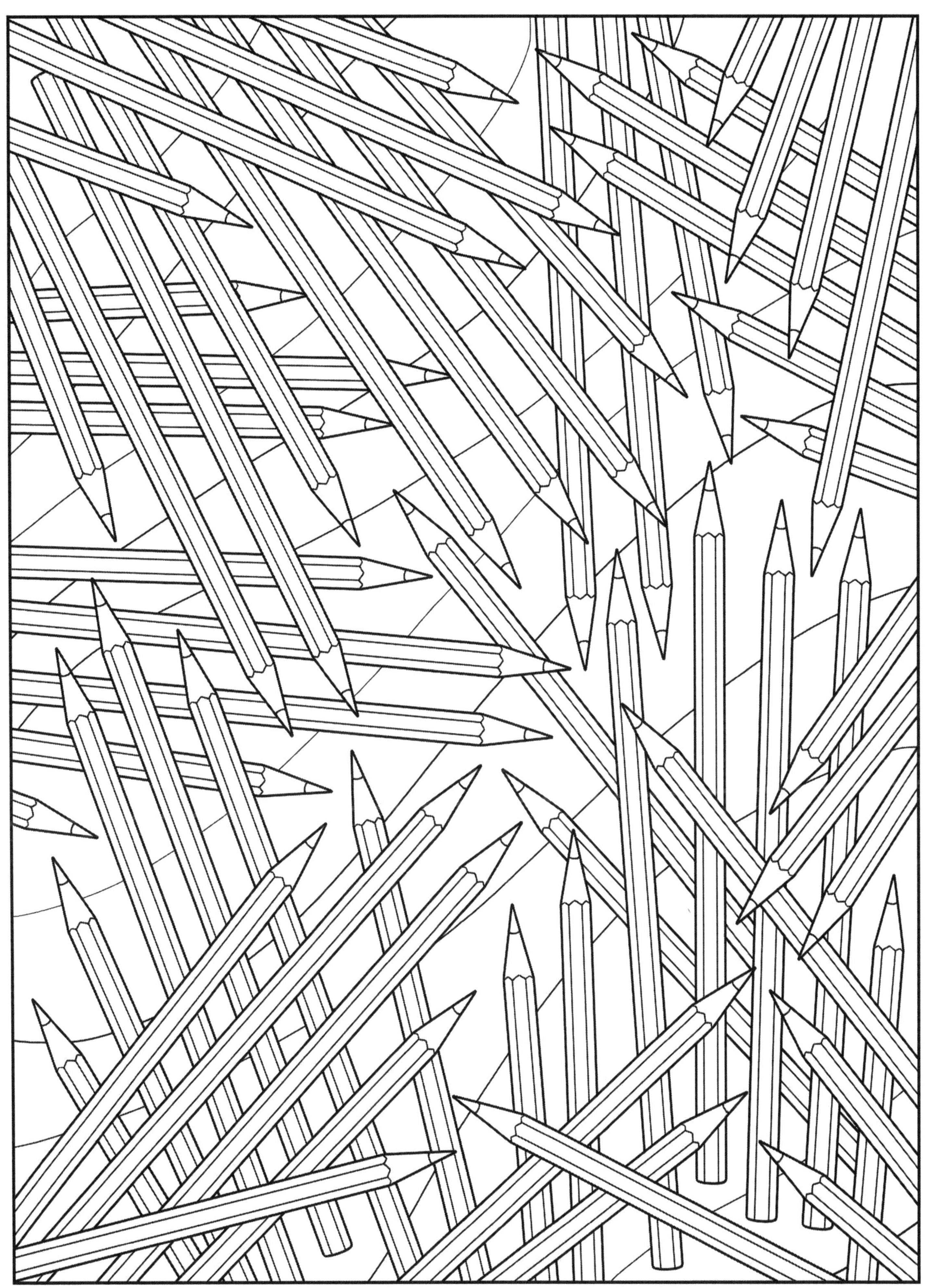

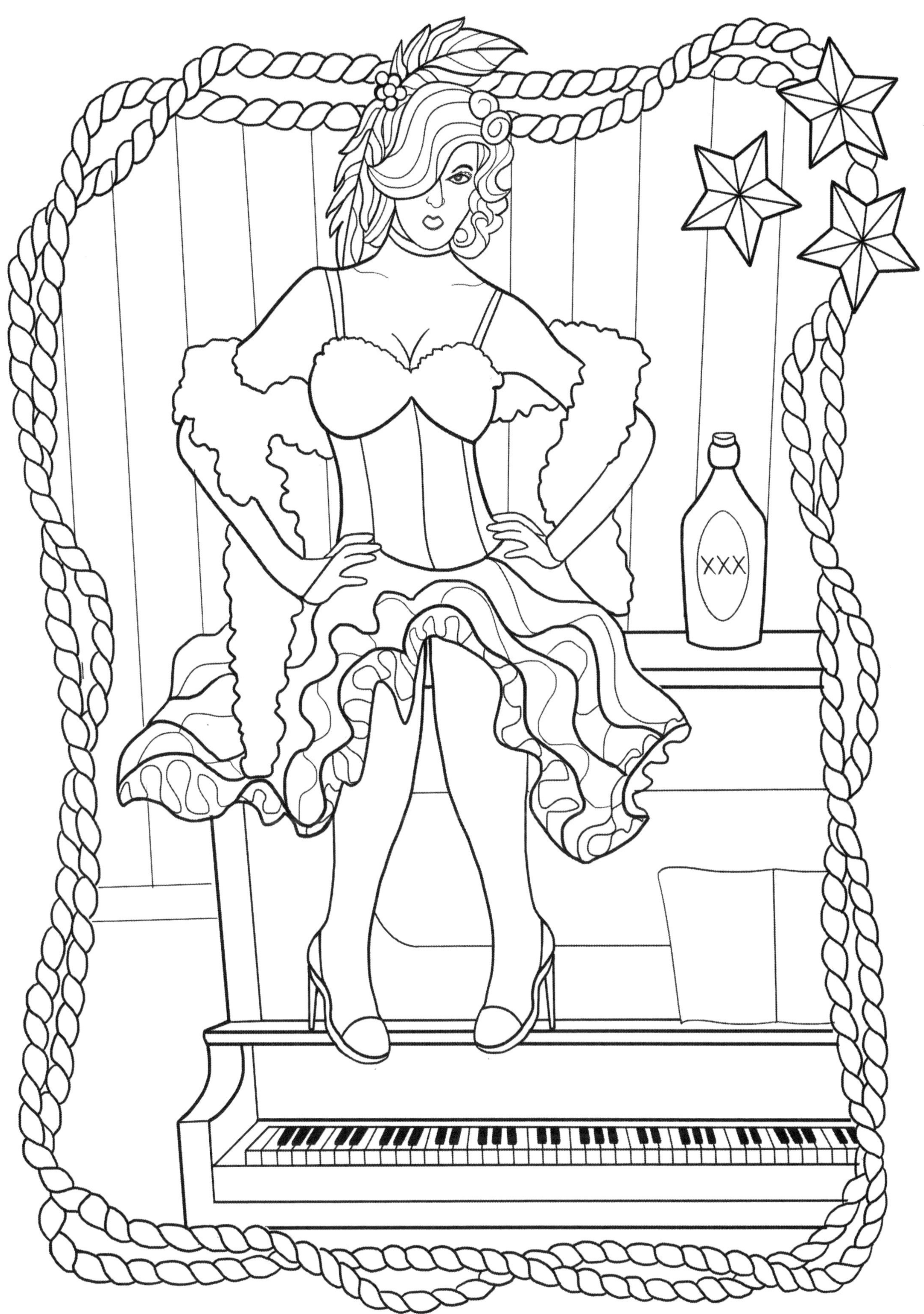
XXX

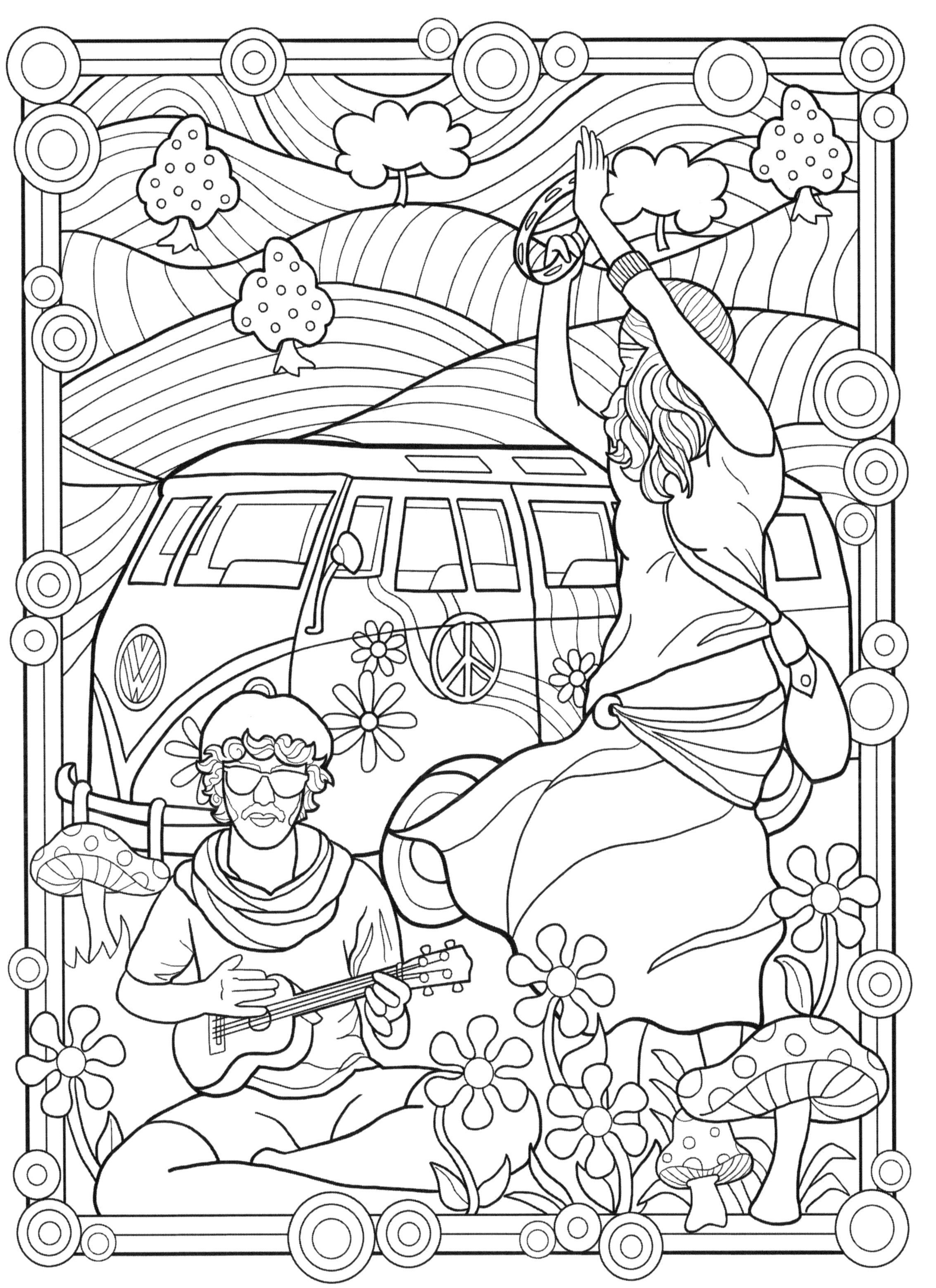

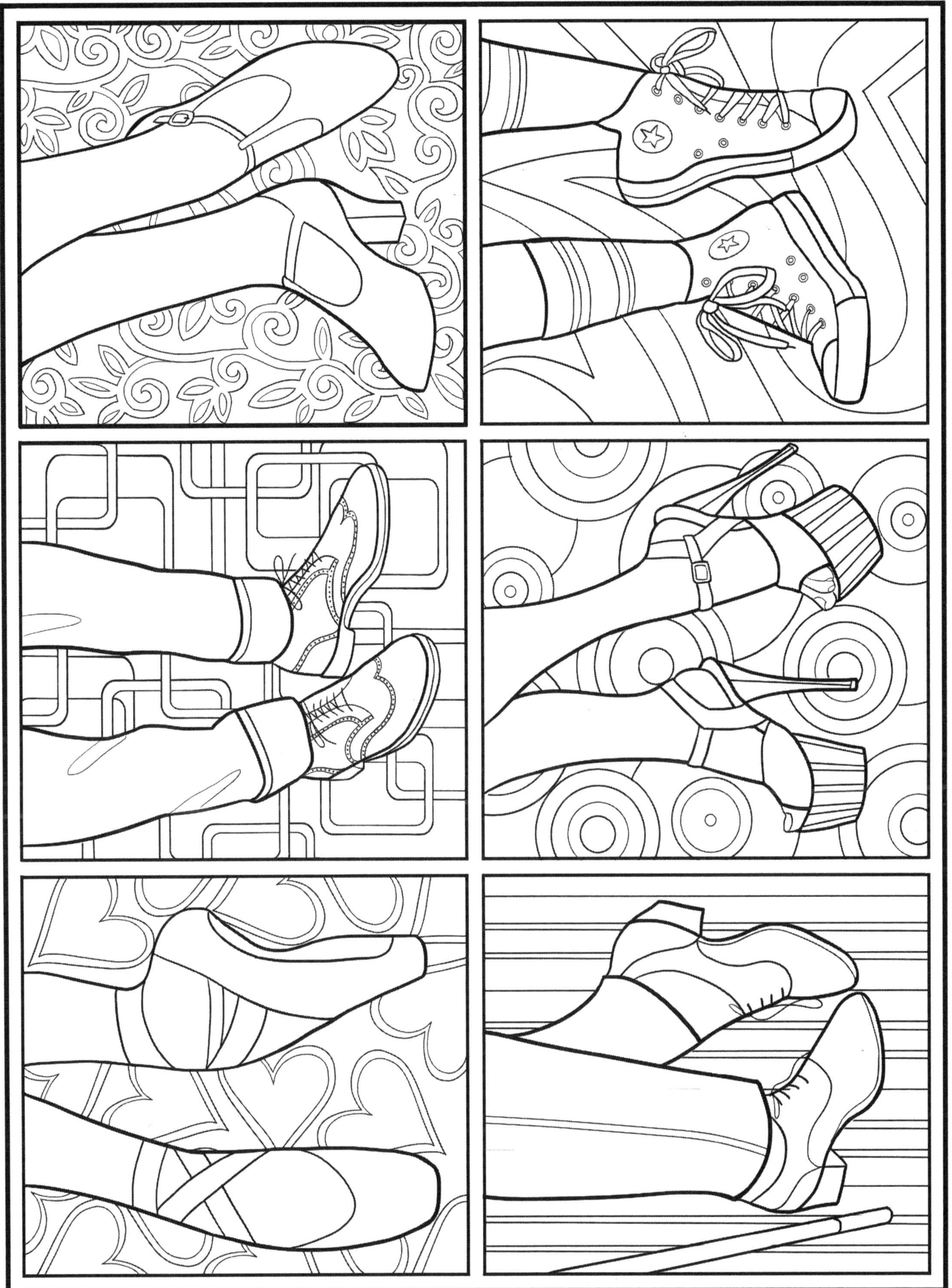

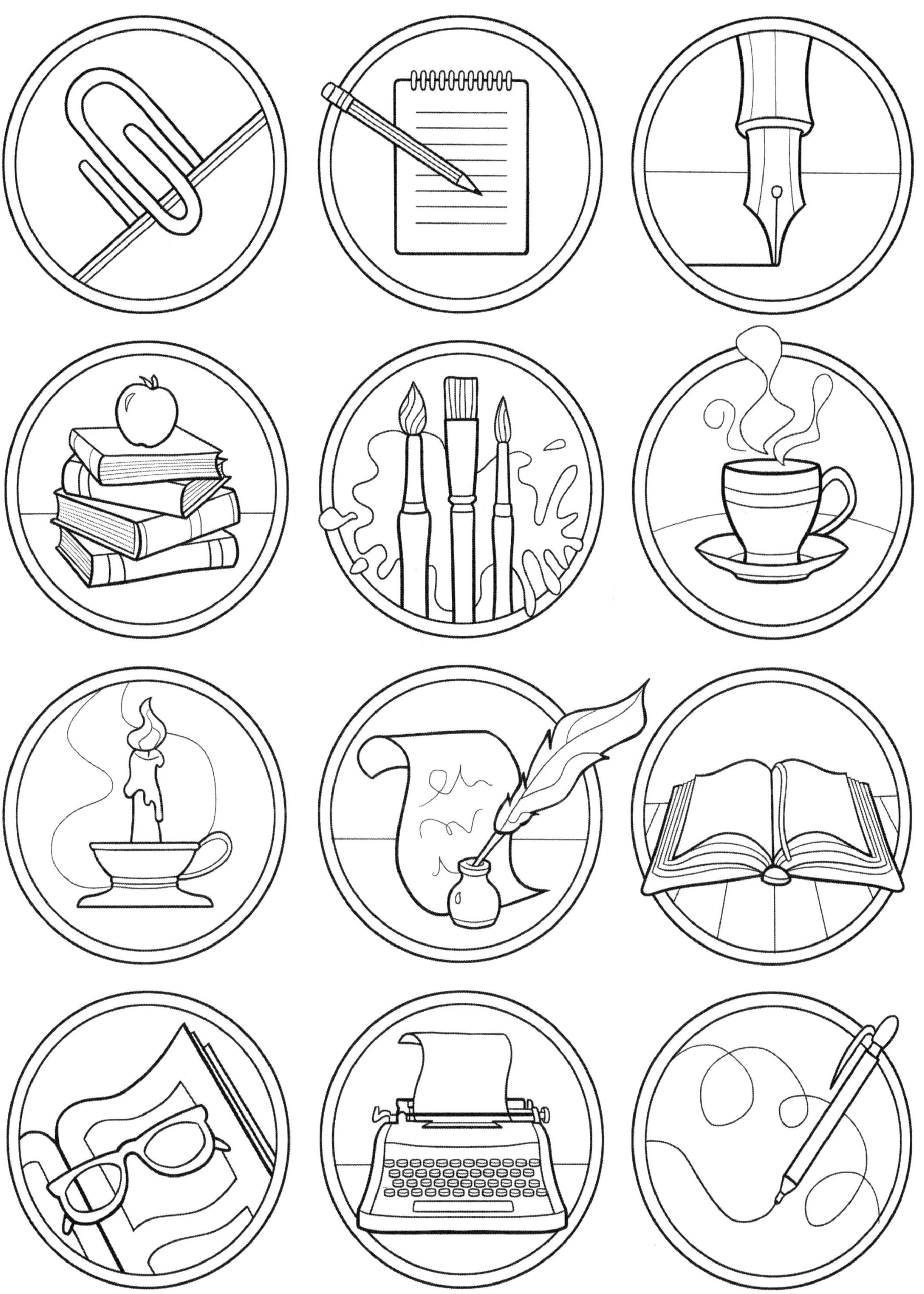

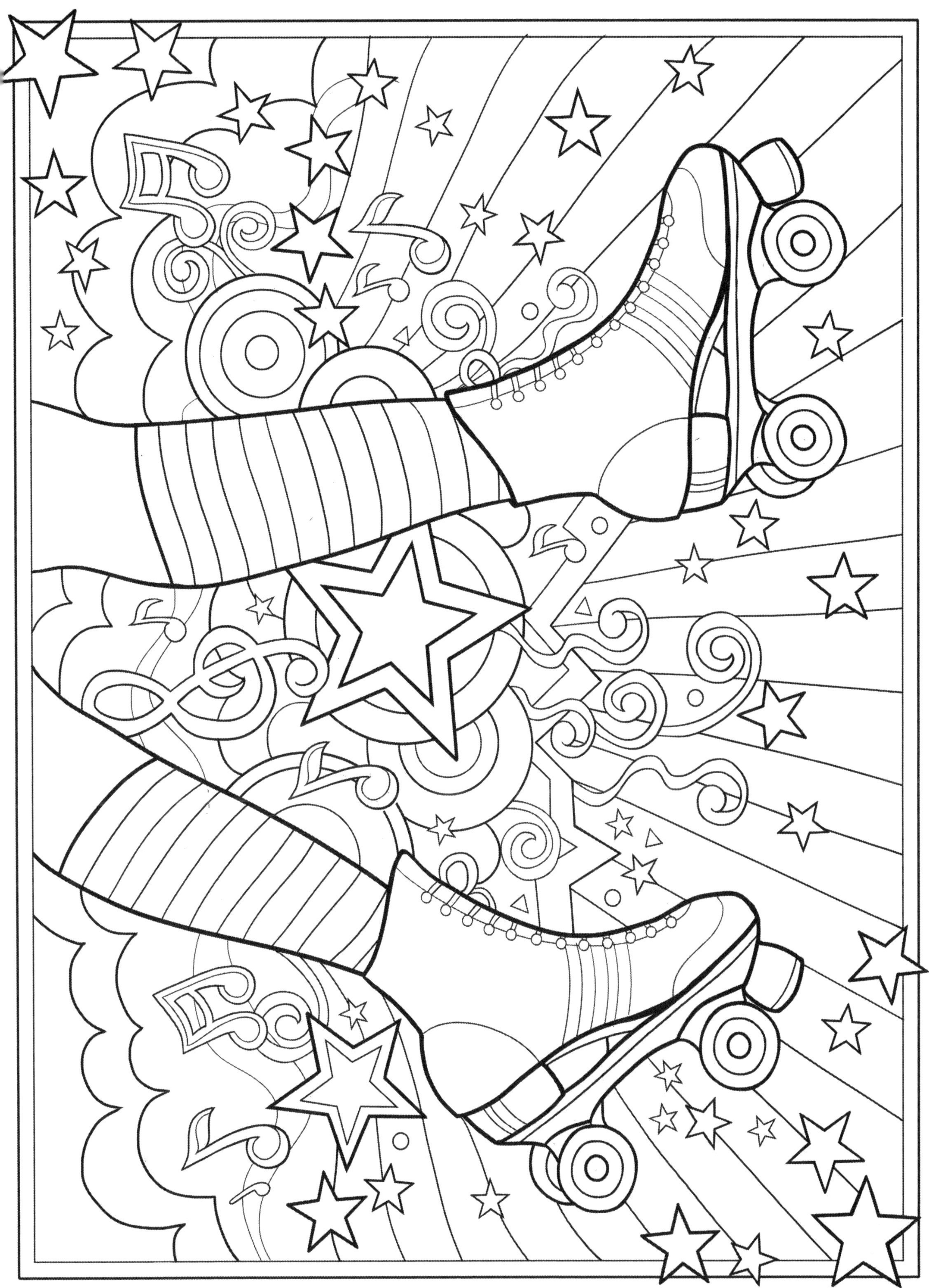

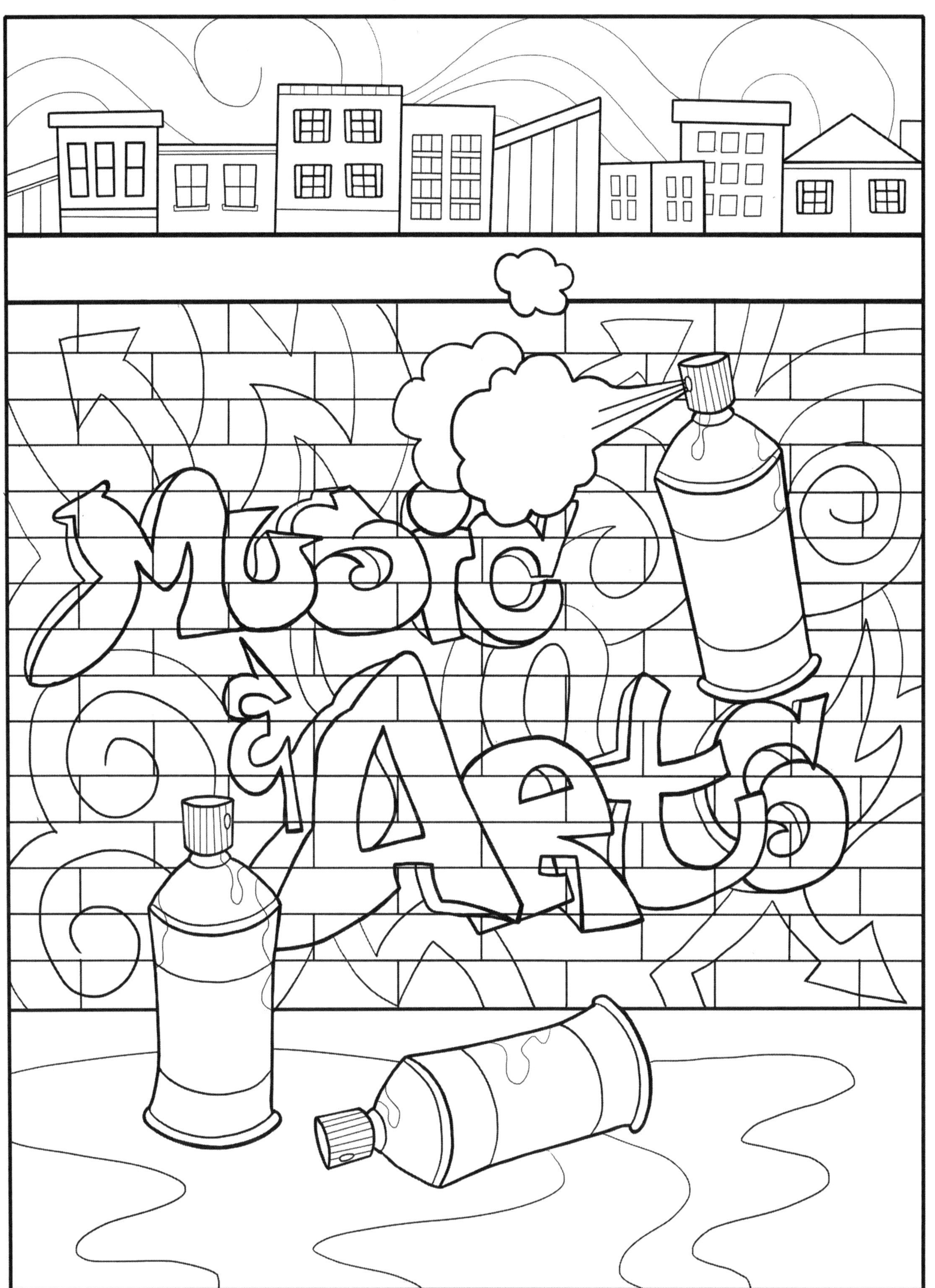
Music
& Arts

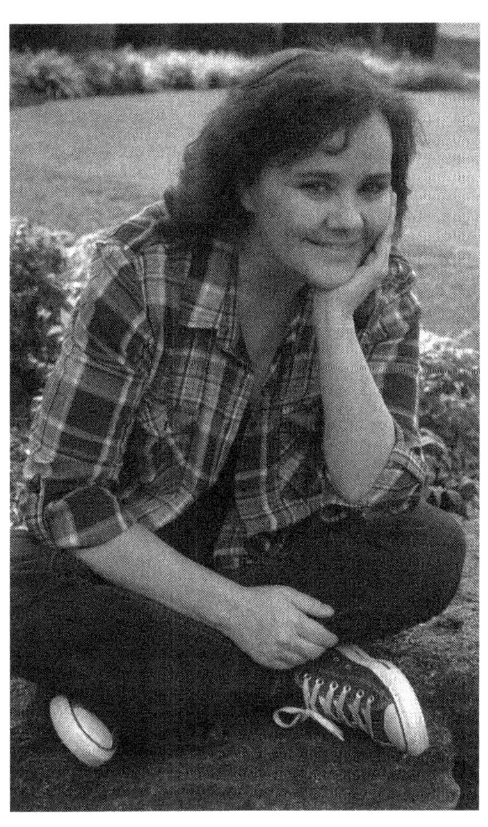

ABOUT THE ARTIST

Jennifer Leigh Allison

Jennifer Leigh Allison is the illustrator of *Flying Colors: An Expert Level Coloring Adventure* and *Flying Colors 2: Music & Arts*. She suffers from a condition known as Sensory Processing Disorder, which is often debilitating and causes a lot of discomfort and everyday challenges. The only activity she has found that truly brings comfort is drawing. As a result, this book was born. It's Jennifer's heart-felt desire to help others find stress relief, focus and fun through the exhilarating experience of coloring.

You can connect with Jennifer online at www.jenniferleighallison.com.

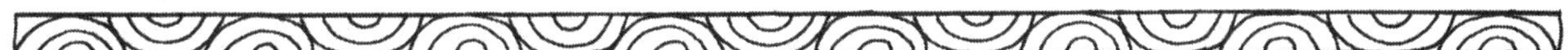

ALSO BY JENNIFER LEIGH ALLISON

Confessions of a Rambunctious Kid

A Quest for Self-Discovery and the Meaning of Life

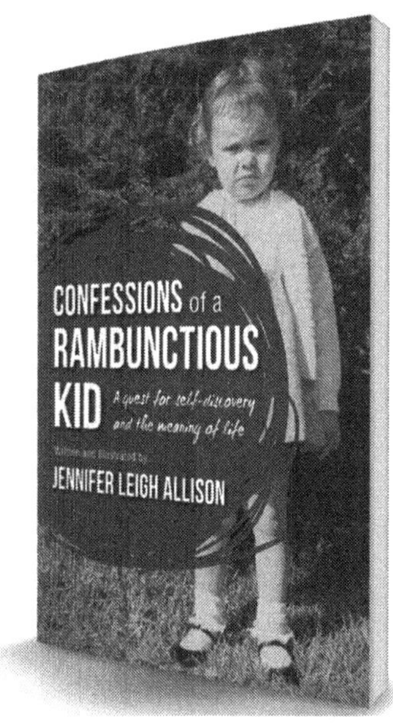

Written with humor and transparency, this nostalgic coming-of-age memoir is about growing up in the south during the '70s and '80s. Jennifer began her quest for self-discovery at an early age when she realized she was different from other kids but didn't know why. She has a unique perspective on life and shares her innermost thoughts and struggles about falling into many deep potholes on her journey, including abuse, addiction, and poverty. Ultimately, however, the challenges taught her some valuable life lessons about who God is. This story will make you laugh, cry, and cheer as you travel alongside Jennifer on the road to hope, transformation, and the meaning of life.

Available at Amazon.com.

Also available for Kindle, Nook, and iBook.

www.ingramcontent.com/pod-product-compliance
Ingram Content Group UK Ltd.
Pitfield, Milton Keynes, MK11 3LW, UK
UKHW051136260726
13967UKWH00010B/3078